A L
Cannon

tales of a lapsed activist

Ted Parker

Dedication

I dedicate this book to my grandchildren for whom it was written in the hope that it proves I was not always a boring old grandfather!

To Isabelle, Reuben, Edward, Theo, Raphael, Adaline, Joshua, Calliope - and any others who arrive in due course.

First published in 2021

Front cover: author addresses the Lewisham anti-NF demonstration 1977.

Back cover: the author in musical mode.

writemark brings publishing into the modern era. Traditional publishers have, and always will be, responsible for bringing some of our greatest writers to the public's attention. They have and always will be constrained by commercial parameters such as print runs and the economy. Now, with the advent of epublishing, this is changing. The only element absent from epublishing is an extraneous affirmation that a work is worth publishing. Now that is also changing. By submitting your manuscript to writemark, our Readers will assess your work and either award you the writemark or provide editorial advice. The writemark logo is a graphic representation of a monkey knot. This was chosen as the organisation's emblem because: 1. It is used to throw lifelines to ships 2. Its name comes from the fact that a monkey, having secured a grasp on something, never lets go and 3. The American hobos used it as a fraternal symbol - it seemed appropriate somehow.

The Sentinel Publishing takes the edited and proof read manuscript and turns it into a hard back, paper back and e book.

Do visit our web site at writemarkweb.wordpress.com

Contents

ACKNOWLEDGEMENTS

I owe the title of this book to my granddaughter Isabelle. Aged four or five at the time she was sitting with her cousin Reuben in a railway cafe, both of them guiltily eating forbidden – and very large – ice creams. When my wife Jennifer came back in after a brief absence and expressed some surprise that they'd been allowed this particular dessert Isabelle remarked that the day out was a treat and, "Anyway, grandad's a loose cannon", a judgement she attributed to her mum, my daughter Emma. This turn of phrase greatly amused me and, on reflection, I have to admit that it's an accurate description, reflecting my disregard for caution in various situations when I should have known better.

That the book's been written at all owes much to my wife, Jennifer, who, noting that it hadn't taken much to distract me from the hard work of writing, constantly encouraged me to return to the task by insisting that mine was a tale worth telling.

I would have got nowhere without the involvement of Bernadette Thompson. I had failed over a number of years to get beyond the few paragraphs I'd strung together following my retirement in 2008.

I decided in September 2019 that my best way forward was to seek out a ghostwriter and I was referred to Bernadette who proved to be admirable in every way. She was perceptive, professional and empathetic. After two lengthy visits she was able to record the details of my long and eventful life and by January 2020 had produced a full-length draft which provided me with the structure and much of the content which I subsequently adapted in order to produce the final book. The lengthy lockdowns of 2020-21 gave me the time and space to finish the job.

By an extraordinary stroke of good fortune, whilst I was working on the book, an old friend, David Cowell, made contact with me after a gap of some 50 years. Jennifer and I were able to meet up with David and his wife, Sue, at their lovely house overlooking the sea at Hythe in Kent in summer 2020. Not only was David able to remind me of a number of half-forgotten episodes from my past but it turned out that he was a brilliant archivist, researcher and – wonder of wonders – book publisher! We were in almost hourly contact throughout as the book project progressed and I am enormously indebted to David for his selfless advice and assistance.

As the rewriting proceeded I felt the need for colleagues who would give me an honest view of whether the material was readable and grammatical. Both Jennifer and David did this superbly but as time went by it was my friend and neighbour Alan Ring who excelled in this role. Alan's working life had been as a civil servant working with prominent politicians and I began to see how meticulous he was when he responded chapter by chapter with detailed corrections and suggestions, resulting in final versions in which I could feel totally confident.

At one point I wanted to check the accuracy of my recollections of the three years I spent in the 94th Entry of RAF electronics apprentices. I turned to Pete Purdy who over the years had been the pivotal person in keeping the ex-members of the 94th in touch by email and periodic reunions.

I am only too aware that my own engagement with the 94th has been somewhat limited. I was therefore enormously grateful when Pete responded so warmly to my request for help and both of us have repeatedly emphasised how rewarding it has been to renew our friendship through this round of correspondence. Pete has shared with me some of his own RAF experiences as well as fascinating details of his early life. It is probably only the pandemic which has kept us from meeting up.

As well as Pete's input I have been grateful for further RAF information from Flash Garratt, Ewan Tennant, Colin Clayton and Roger Todd.

As with the RAF years I needed to check recollections and accuracy from my time at Barking College. The number of colleagues there actually runs into hundreds but I settled for three who could remind me of some of what I'd forgotten. I'd like to offer apologies to all those I didn't contact – but I'm very grateful for the kind and helpful responses of those I did ask – Chris Witt, Mike Rowton and Andrew Brader. They are all representative in their different ways of the positive 'can-do' spirit which made the place a joy to work in.

I am grateful for the support of my immediate family who are so precious to me. Similarly, I greatly appreciate the renewed contact with and kind encouragement of an old friend, Morgan O'Brien, who crops up from time to time in the story and who has stayed true to his early radicalism even as my views have shifted with the changing times.

Chapter 1

A War Baby

I was born during the Second World War on 31st October 1943 and was brought up on the Kent coast in Folkestone, across the English Channel from France. As a youngster I was drawn to the seaside – particularly Folkestone's picturesque harbour. In the 1950's it was graced with colourful fishing boats, evidence of its part in the country's then-thriving fishing industry. I swam from the beaches and wandered the clifftops between Folkestone and Dover where military relics such as pillboxes remained as reminders of the recent threat of invasion.

The town had been shelled by the Germans on a regular basis throughout the war from a gun emplacement at Wissant, a resort on the French coast near Calais.

During my early years my mum was full of stories of what had gone on during the war. Folkestone and the adjacent coast were known as Hell's Corner because of the concentration of bombs dropped there, presumably jettisoned by German bombers unable to get through to other targets. She continually told me tales of what she had seen – the waves of German bombers, the dogfights between British and German fighter planes, many crashing in flames, and occasional parachutes coming down.

She even recalled being dragged away from a bedroom window by my dad when she called him to look at a Spitfire hurtling down the street at rooftop level only to realize that it was a German Messerschmitt which then started machine-gunning. Before that she had been in Ramsgate and seen the small boats returning to the Kent coast with injured and bedraggled survivors from Dunkirk.

The heroism of the Battle of Britain pilots made a great impression on me and I was determined that when I grew up I was going to join the Royal Air Force, as a pilot if I could.

My dad was an army motorcycle despatch rider, part of the Allied forces that invaded France on D-Day. His accounts of the horrors he'd seen in the Nazi concentration camps liberated by the Allies were related to me in the following years by my mother, and images of the Holocaust have affected my whole outlook on life. I have always been an active anti-racist, and I loathe tyranny, whether of the political Left or, as with the Nazis, of the Right.

When the war ended in 1945 my dad stayed in Berlin as part of the occupation forces, but he was able to visit us from time to time. I remember that whenever he came home on leave he would laughingly swing me and my mum off our feet. I'll always remember how happy I was when he turned up, sometimes without warning. He finally returned home for good about the time my sister Jean was born on 25th February 1948, and that should have marked the beginning of a long-awaited family life together.

Instead, within a year, he was diagnosed with Hodgkin's Disease and was admitted to hospital. Hodgkin's Disease is a cancer that nowadays is treatable, but in those days it was fatal, and people with Hodgkin's were put straight into isolation because of the risk of spreading the infection. My sister and I weren't allowed to visit him, but I do remember standing outside his hospital window one day, and then mum lifting me up so that I could see him. Not long after that, mum left Jean and me with my grandmother while she went to see dad. When she came back, she was in tears; she said something like, "Dad has died. He's gone up to heaven to be with the angels." He was 32. It was 1950.

I was six years old and devastated. For weeks afterwards I stared at the glass in my bedroom window and prayed for my dad's face to materialise, or that he would float past like some sort of angel. I wished and wished that he wasn't dead, and I constantly prayed that God would bring him back to us.

It had a huge impact on me. It's true that I'd hardly known him because he'd been away fighting a war, so people thought it wouldn't matter that much to me, but he was my dad, he'd always been there somewhere, and now he was gone, and it mattered enormously.

My mum felt it best that my sister and I should not attend the funeral, being so young, but later she brought Jean and me to the cemetery. It was in Minster, a little Kent village near Ramsgate, where my mum had first lived. I can recall holding tightly to some flowers and standing at the graveside. There was a chill wind, and it was all very quiet.

Then, in the distance, there was the whine of a motorbike engine and I immediately thought, "That's my dad!" The sound of that bike, right then, was like my dad paying me a visit. I remember it vividly to this day. There was no headstone on his grave and, in retrospect, I can see that we were quite poor, though throughout our childhood my mum made sure we had no real awareness of this.

When it came to registering dad's death there was a problem because nobody could find the birth certificate to match his name, Edward Parker. Within a couple of days of his death, his parents came down from Hull, where my dad had been born, and mum asked about the birth certificate. That was when the Parkers said, "Well, that's because his name was Lewis Clubley".

This was news to my mum – and it would have been news to my dad too. It seems amazing that he had been able to join the army without proof of identity but there we are. He died believing he was Edward Parker. I was named after him. But the people I thought were my grandparents, Edwin and Grace Parker, weren't my grandparents at all.

This mystery always intrigued me but it wasn't until the 1980's that I finally got round to finding some answers. By then I had lost touch with the Parkers, despite them sending me Christmas presents whilst I was still a small child. I obtained a copy of the long version of my dad's birth certificate. There was no father listed, but his mother's name was Annis Clubley and three addresses were specified. One was her place of work - a pub where she was a barmaid. The second turned out to be a workhouse where unmarried mothers were admitted to have their babies and the last was a road in Hull where she lived.

I wondered if Annis had subsequently got married and if I could track her down from that. It transpired that she had indeed got married – to Wilfred Clark - in 1923 and had a daughter named Winifred. Winifred got married in 1945 to Walter Howard. The Howards subsequently moved to London and had three sons. At the time of my research they were all living in West London. I managed to make contact and, to my astonishment, found out that Annis was still alive, aged 89, and living in a village called Patrington, between Hull and the mysterious and isolated coastal promontory of Spurn Head.

One of the brothers, Ed Howard, had recently moved up to Patrington with his wife, Kerry, and I got his address. I then made the long journey up north with my then wife, Britt and our two very young children, Emma and Joel. We stayed with friends of Britt's in Grimsby for a few days. I travelled back and forth over the Humber Bridge to Hull to try to track down Annis. I first called on Ed and Kerry who, though very welcoming, were unwilling to give me Annis' address for fear of upsetting her. However, I persevered and, after some early difficulties, got to see her sister, May, her niece Hilda and finally Annis herself.

May, then aged about 87, confided to me that before Annis got married she had already had three children. She said "Two died and we don't know what happened to the third one". I soon found out!

I had been surprised, on first driving into Patrington, to see various businesses badged up as 'Clubley', a name I had only come across in relation to my dad. There was a Clubley garage and, in the middle of the village, a Clubley general store. On the second day of my quest I called into the store on the off-chance to ask the woman serving if she happened to know the whereabouts of Annis Clark as she was called by then. She responded immediately by saying "She lives opposite – I'll introduce you". We went across. The door was unlocked and we went straight in. The woman from the shop said "Mrs. Clark, there's someone to see you". I went into the front room and there was this delightful old lady with blue eyes and white hair sitting by the fire. She told me to come in and sit down.

I told her my tale: " I'm Ted Parker and my dad was called Ted Parker – but it turned out that that was not his real name – his real name was Lewis Clubley". "Oh", Annis replied "My brother was Lewis."

"No" I said, "that Lewis would be too old. My dad was born in 1918, and his mum was called Annis Clubley. There was only one Annis Clubley born at the right time and that's you, and I think you're my grandmother." She slowly shook her head and her expression became wistful. It was immediately obvious to me that she wasn't going to let me pursue the matter but that she was nevertheless the right person. Ed and Kerry Howard, with whom I kept up an occasional correspondence, later confirmed this.

After seeing Annis I went back to Grimsby and followed up one final lead. I had a record of an acquaintance of the Parkers who coincidentally lived in Grimsby and I went there unannounced to find, to my astonishment, that they had a photo of me and my sister Jean, aged six and two respectively, when our mum had taken us to Hull to talk to the Parkers immediately after my dad's death in 1950. They had stayed friendly with the Parkers until their deaths several years later. They told me that in 1918 the Parkers had lived near to Annis and had become aware that her first two children had died. They somehow persuaded Annis to let them take her third child to avoid him suffering the same fate. I have in my possession a document signed by the Parkers in 1936 confirming that the young man living with them and known as Edward Parker was born in 1918 and registered as Lewis Clubley. As detailed earlier, my dad had not known any of this.

Getting back to my own early years – they are all to do with the Kent coast to which I have always felt a strong attachment. My mum's family were from Ramsgate originally. Most of them ended up as laundry workers. Before I was born my mum and gran moved to Folkestone, where I spent all my early years.

When my dad died my mum was in a difficult position because not only did my dad leave no money, but through having been involved in trying to set up a mobile laundry business he had left debts. Someone had cheated him out of the cost of a van or something. I can remember later on in my life seeing a van going around where I used to live in Folkestone. On the side was written Sandgate Laundries, and my mum used to say, "That's the firm your dad set up." Anyway, mum really struggled financially. She worked hard and was a very proud woman; she wouldn't dream of claiming any benefits. She spent her life either as a cleaner or working in laundries. In the years following my dad's death she lived frugally, carefully keeping the money for the various bills in separate labeled tins in the kitchen.

One time my mum sent Jean and me to the grocery shop on the corner of our street; I must have been about seven, possibly eight, and I remember standing there with my little sister in front of the grocer, asking for what we needed - probably basics such as bread and milk. On the counter was a display of sweets. As the grocer handed over our purchases Jean said, "Eddie, can we have some sweets?" I can clearly remember looking directly at the grocer and saying in a firm voice, "Jean, we can't afford sweets." I picked up our shopping and turned to leave. With that the grocer took a handful of sweets, put them in a paper bag and gave them to me. As politely as possible I said "Thank you very much" and walked calmly out of the shop before returning home to tell mum of our great good fortune.

As we got older, there were other things that I noticed. I must have been about eleven when I found out that some youngsters got a thing called 'pocket money', and went to a thing called 'Saturday Morning Pictures'. It made you realise that life was not entirely fair. However, things were about to change for the better.

Mum was a cleaner at the military hospital at the nearby Shorncliffe army camp and one day a fellow-passenger on the bus offered to pay her fare. He was called Arthur Ashby and worked at the camp as a telephone operator. One thing led to another and in due course they got married, by which time I was thirteen. I remember being a bit jealous of someone else sharing my mum's affections and he made a big effort to persuade me and Jean that we should welcome him into our household. A decisive factor was when he said "I'll be bringing my television". This was 1956 and a television was an unimaginable luxury. After that, his welcome was assured!

He turned out to be a very kind and thoughtful stepfather. This was the era of rock'n roll and I must have mentioned that I'd have liked to have a guitar. I came in one day and was told to go into the front room where – to my complete surprise – there was a brand-new guitar! I was told that it was mine as long as I took lessons to learn how to play it properly. I've never looked back. I'd formed a skiffle group within weeks and have never subsequently been without a guitar. I played rock'n roll when Elvis was in the ascendancy, folk music when Dylan arrived and have never been at a loss to perform at social gatherings ever since.

I haven't mentioned my education. I enjoyed primary school – a delightful establishment called Harcourt, subsequently renamed Pent Valley, round the corner at the bottom of our road. All the teachers were very kind and caring.

I recollect gaining a certain prominence by performing two particular roles. I was obsessed with the radio and I somehow found myself with the duty of writing the day's forthcoming Children's Hour programmes on the blackboard every morning. The other, somewhat more unusual task, also related the radio. There was a performer called Percy Edwards who had made a career out of imitating animal noises. I found that this was an ability that I myself possessed and before long I was assigned to touring all the classrooms making the diverse sounds of the farmyard. I quite enjoyed all this and would happily have continued in the same way throughout my school career. However, unfortunately the children were streamed by ability as they got older. There were two streams and I found myself in the one for the less able children. Clearly, making animal noises was not a talent which attracted the recognition it deserved.

My mum made me aware that being assigned to the lower stream meant it was unlikely that I would get into the grammar school when I became eleven. It is hard now, following the subsequent widespread adoption of comprehensive education, to understand how all-consuming was the anxiety of parents to get their children into grammar schools rather than the much-maligned secondary moderns. Grammar schools were seen as for the managerial classes whilst the secondary moderns were for manual workers. Meanwhile the Technical Schools, which should have provided the country with a cadre of industrial and scientific technicians, were a neglected and largely missing element of the so-called tripartite post-war education system.

My mum drilled into me the importance of the forthcoming 'eleven-plus' exams which would determine which children got into grammar schools. Suddenly, some months before these exams, my spirits lifted when a pupil from the higher stream left the school, leaving a vacancy in his class. After some debate I got his place and moved up to where expectations were much higher and coaching was geared accordingly.

As I was sitting in the eleven-plus exam writing the answers the head-teacher, Mr. Regan, was walking round the hall and at one point stopped behind me and whispered "Go faster Eddie". Whether I managed it or not I can't remember but on the day the results were announced I was as anxious as everyone else. My mum was hopeful but had nevertheless checked the price of the uniform at Morehall Secondary School. One of my friends had a school-teacher father who had already assumed he would be going to the grammar school. What a shock when the results came out – I got through and my friend didn't. However, his family very quickly secured his place at a prestigious private school – class always finds a way!

So, somewhat against the odds, I had managed to get into Harvey Grammar School, founded in 1674 by the family of Dr William Harvey, the first person to explain the circulation of blood in the human body. There's a large statue of him in Folkestone near the seafront at the end of a fashionable road called Clifton Gardens. Our 'school song' asserted 'In times ne'er forgotten the Founder established it' and required us to acknowledge "the name and the fame of our time-honoured school".

However, my own time there was not very happy. Again, all the classes were streamed by academic ability. I was rapidly relegated to the bottom class. Nor was this all. At the end of each year the form teacher gave out the results, calling out the name of the pupils and their scores, beginning at the top, in front of the whole class. This would go on remorselessly, all the way down to the person with the lowest score at the bottom, and that was me, and not only was I bottom, I was bottom by a vast amount!

Years later I realised it was not all to do with intelligence but also with the lottery of upbringing. Then, as now, working class children have the educational cards stacked against them. In those days girls suffered particularly from a lack of places in girls' grammar schools. My sister Jean seemed to withdraw into herself when she failed the eleven-plus exam and was sent to a secondary modern school. My dislike of selection with its separation of children into successes and failures stems from that time.

Not only did I do badly academically but I was no good at sports and I also experienced various petty humiliations from time to time. For instance, though I was good at English and thought I was getting on well with the English teacher, 'Soapy' Huston, there was an occasion when I fell foul of him for no real reason. He began one of his lessons by reading from a book which started "It was the 31st October". He put the book down and asked "What is 31st October?"

I was aware that this wouldn't be the answer he expected but, struck by the coincidence of it being my birthday, I put my hand up, envisaging a generally humorous response from all concerned to my, clearly wrong, answer. Before allowing me to reply Mr. Huston said "Hold on Parker, give the others a chance". On going round the class and getting no other suggestions (in those days there was no celebration of Halloween) he finally said "OK Parker, give them the answer". I said "It's my birthday Sir". With that he coldly said "Come out here and hold your hand out" and then administered four painful swipes of the cane on my palm. I imagine that the lesson then continued with a description of Halloween but, to be honest, I would have lost interest by then.

Another time I got beaten round the head with a large hard-back book by a Geography teacher – Mr. Nichols – because, though I'd spent the entire previous evening carefully drawing a map of Australia, I'd ruined it because I'd decided I could provide the finishing touch by colouring it in but we only had a thick black crayon at home and it ended up looking terrible.

Another bizarre encounter took place in the gym. The PE teacher, 'Killer' Howard, had allegedly been an instructor in the Navy and believed in strict discipline based on fear. Much of our time in the gym was spent standing to attention in teams, in total silence, dressed in white shorts and vests, whilst he lectured us on various of his obsessions such as having clean feet.

On one such occasion a pupil in the team standing opposite us in the gym started laughing. Mr. Howard said "Pass" (the boy's name) "why are you laughing?" He said "Because Newble was laughing Sir". "Newble, why were you laughing?". "Because Parker was pulling a funny face Sir". I had not been, and immediately said so. The teacher said "I'll show you what happens to boys who pull faces in my class". He then made me bend over in the middle of the gym, got a large rubber slipper and gave me six mighty swipes on my backside.

Things continued in much the same way. There was the time when my class had been taken to Folkestone Town Hall to see a play being performed in French – presumably to help us to learn the language. Unfortunately I could not understand a word - neither could the rest of the class as far as I could see because to amuse themselves they started taking off the clips which connected the rows of tubular chairs to each other. Needless to say I did the same. At the end of the play I put my clips back on the chairs. Clearly not everyone did because some time later back at the school the headmaster addressed the pupils and asked who had taken the clips off the chairs. I put up my hand but few, if any, of the others did. I had no chance to tell him that I had put the clips back before I was marched into his office for a caning, presumably to placate the town hall caretaker who would have faced the onerous task of putting the clips back himself. Not long after this I was again caned by the headteacher because a teacher had come off his bike when colliding with me on his way home from school.

As I seemed unable to do anything right at school I took great pleasure in outside activities. I enjoyed my guitar and also loved my bike, spending lots of time cycling to the beach and swimming. My best friend was Chris Renham whose dad owned a bike shop so we were forever modifying our bikes with different saddles and handle bars and doing tricks such as standing on the saddles whilst riding. These are among the fondest memories of my early teenage years – and, of course, listening endlessly to rock'n roll on records and Radio Luxemburg. Oh – and the comedy programme Hancock's Half Hour on the BBC. On a more serious note, I joined the 99th Squadron of the Air Training Corps (ATC) in pursuit of my ambition to join the RAF.

Given that I was probably one of the worst pupils at Harvey Grammar it says much for the school that I managed to scrape a creditable four 'O' levels (equivalent to modern-day GCSE's). They were in English Literature, English Language, Maths, and – somewhat surprisingly – Geography. I can only think that I achieved a pass in Geography because, by our final year, we had the most friendly and considerate teacher I can recall – Gerry Holmes, who was unique in calling us by our first names and who took the trouble to work with us individually to make sure we understood things.

English and Maths were based on principles with which I had no real trouble. But I struggled to grasp certain other subjects, particularly the sciences, which means I need now to explain how I subsequently found myself training to become an electronics technician. In those days you could leave school at 15 by which time you would normally have taken 'O' levels. Pupils with good 'O' level results would have been expected to stay on into the school's sixth form to take 'A' levels and possibly go on to University. For many this would have been an impossible dream and for my part it was not even a consideration. However, there were other opportunities.

It was 1959, a time of full employment. Compulsory National Service was coming to an end and the three military services were making great efforts to make up their numbers by encouraging young people to sign up voluntarily. Harvey Grammar would have been ideal territory and the pupils were encouraged to attend recruitment interviews. I had no hesitation in heading for the Royal Air Force display and talking to one of the RAF recruiters seated at a table.

He asked me what interested me in the RAF and I explained that I had been inspired by its role during the war and had joined the Air Training Corps some years before, choosing the aircrew option. I said that I would have liked to be a pilot but that based on my school experience I was aware that I would not be suitable.

He asked me why not and I can remember saying "You have to be very fit and very bright and I'm not either". He said I might be under-valuing myself but I said I didn't think so and added "If I can't be a pilot, what other options would I have?" He said "Well, the next best thing would be an electronics apprenticeship". He put my name on the list and just after Christmas I found myself in the 94th Entry of Air Force Apprentices at the RAF's No. 1 Radio School, RAF Locking, Weston-Super-Mare, Somerset, having been signed up, with my parents' agreement, till the age of 30. I was 16 years old.

Chapter 2

Royal Air Force – a career cut short

I joined the Royal Air Force at the age of sixteen in January 1960, part of the 94th Entry of Air Force Apprentices at RAF Locking, the RAF's No.1 Radio School located near the seaside resort of Weston-Super-Mare in Somerset. There were about seventy of us in the 94th Entry. Like civilian schools, study was broken down into three terms a year with an 'Entry' being the cohort joining each term – summer, winter and spring.

Summer entries were the largest, with entrants recruited from summer school leavers. The 94th, being a winter entry, was relatively small. Entries were grouped into squadrons, with winter entries in "A" Squadron. A strong squadron identity was encouraged, as was 'Entry Spirit' through such things as sport and drill competitions as well as many unofficial schemes and pranks.

The 94th Entry was housed in four long interconnected huts which each held about twenty people. Each of us had a bed, a small wooden locker for personal effects and a tall metal locker for our uniforms and rifles. In charge were Apprentice Non-Commissioned Officers (NCO's) from senior entries in our own squadron. As time went by the more promising members of our own entry were selected to be NCO's and incorporated into the disciplinary structure.

In our three years together we got to know each other really well. There were people from all sorts of backgrounds which broadened my horizons considerably. In my hut alone there was Paddy McCauley from Northern Ireland, Doug Bradley and Jock Sergison from Scotland and Dai Davies from Wales.

Then there were those from the big cities – Mike McKenna from Manchester, Chippy Wood from Leeds and Dave Kirk from Liverpool. Kirk, I later found out, went on to have a fascinating career in Special Forces. In one of many incidents he was on the point of arresting leading IRA terrorist Martin McGuinness when he was instructed by radio to let him go because the British government secretly needed him free to progress the Peace Process.

We had two colleagues from the Ceylon Air Force - Cyril Siriwadane and Widgie Guneratna. Then there were those whose leadership qualities led to early promotion – among them Pete Purdy, Geoff Hadley and Dave Kitching. I also developed close friendships with some fellow rock'n roll fans and we put together a band comprising Mike "Flash" Garratt (and later Johny Bates) on rhythm guitar, Mick Crewe on bass guitar, Olly Holbrook (and later Norman 'Lefty' Wright, from Southern Rhodesia) on drums and myself on lead guitar and vocals. We were joined from time to time by Geoff Hadley on vocals. We called ourselves the Whirlwinds – later the Skid Row Combo – and played to considerable acclaim at concerts in the camp – and once, astonishingly, at a hall in Bristol where Gene Vincent had played a few weeks earlier!
In later years unofficial trips to Bristol – strictly

speaking out of bounds – became highlights because we could go to the Colston Hall (latterly renamed) to see rock'n roll stars such as Gene Vincent, Jerry Lee Lewis and Joe Brown.

When we first got to Locking the daily routine took some getting used to. We were woken at 6am by a tannoy in each hut ordering us to get up followed by a programme of pop music – one song which sticks in my head even now, a lifetime later, is 'One way ticket to the blues' which summed up how I felt 200 miles from home with no easy way back! After speedy ablutions we had kit inspections – kit needed to be laid out on our beds in a particular pattern – then we lined up on parade outside for a further inspection before we were marched off for breakfast. Then we had a full day of drill, physical education and technical training before being marched back to our huts for an evening of cleaning our kit and polishing the floors.

I think we all found it tough but were determined to stick it out. The whole regime had been refined for many years by the air force to ensure they ended up with the kind of person they wanted. As a result, most of us developed enormous pride in the RAF and particularly the 94th Entry.

There was a delightful interlude when I heard from home that there was a new addition to the family – my mum gave birth to my brother David on 4th July 1960 – and I was able to secure a 48-hour pass on compassionate grounds to dash across the country to see him. Strictly speaking he was my half-brother. My step-father treated me and my sister Jean brilliantly but he yearned for a child of his own and, together, we made a great family – the new family name was Ashby though I chose to hang onto Parker – but more of family life later.

Meanwhile at Locking there was a dimension to apprentice life back then that I hadn't expected, and that was institutionalised bullying by the senior entries within our own squadron. What happened was that at the dead of night the doors of our huts would burst open and a crowd of people would come in and start pulling us out of bed and shouting at us. That was part of what was called 'Senior Entryism' which was an established tradition to take away the newest recruits and make them work in the senior entries' huts overnight, polishing floors and cleaning their kit. It was pretty unpleasant, especially as we were already exhausted from the normal arduous day's activities. We didn't know how to react because if we fought back we were likely to come off worst. We were sixteen years old and the senior entry intruders were two years older. Also, the apprentice NCOs in charge of our huts were from those same senior entries and supported what was going on.

In the 94th Entry with me, but in a different hut, was a bloke called Mike McKenna. We got to know each other well. He was from the Langley Estate which, I got to know later, was a tough working-class area in Middleton, Manchester. McKenna did fight back. When they came into his hut he was holding two broken bottles in his hands, daring them to come at him. Unable to drag him away, they took his kit and threw it all over the camp. When it came to the next morning's kit inspection he didn't have any kit to lay out. He was put on a charge for not having his kit and given punishment duties, which we called Jankers, or Janks.

Soon his notoriety grew further. Whenever an Apprentice NCO came into the hut, we had to shout "NCO" and all stand to attention until we were told to carry on. On one occasion as the NCO went out, McKenna threw a knife at the door, but the NCO hadn't quite closed it, and the knife flew past him. It hit the corridor wall with a clatter. The door slowly swung back open, and there was a very ashen-faced NCO standing there. He said "Who threw that?" No-one replied, but heads turned towards McKenna. "Right" said the NCO, "you've done it now McKenna".

The apprentices were a law unto themselves, so it wasn't necessary to invoke official RAF disciplinary procedures.The next we knew was that, as a result of a conference of NCOs, it was decided to charge McKenna with a newly invented offence: 'Attempting to reduce Her Majesty's Forces'. We laughed when we heard that. It was better than attempted murder! As a result, McKenna was put on punishment duties for months on end.

Later on, whilst once again on punishment duties, he pretended to be ill so he could get put into the sick bay. Whilst there he said he wanted to have a bath, but instead of getting in, arranged for someone else to replace him. Whenever any of the supervisory staff called out "Where's McKenna?" someone would say, "He's in the bath" and any further enquiry would be met by a confirmatory reply from behind the bathroom door. In the meantime, McKenna would be out on the town, enjoying himself drinking, probably in a pub called The

Captain's Cabin near Weston-Super-Mare's seafront. I must say that not withstanding his humble origins he was one of the brightest and most enterprising people I ever met.

On another occasion he master-minded an illegal but highly effective 94th Entry coup. Once a year some of Locking's apprentices got to spend a week at RAF St. Mawgan in Cornwall, and had a chance to visit the nearby seaside resort of Newquay. On one such occasion our squadron's senior entry, the 91st, had managed to steal a large spherical naval mine from the town's esplanade and somehow got it back to Locking. It became a prized trophy.

When the 91st Entry completed their training and left Locking in December 1961 the mine was bequeathed to the 94th. However, it was subsequently captured by 'B' Squadron's 92nd Entry, placed outside one of their huts and carefully guarded with the help of booby-traps comprising ropes attached to the mine and fixed to metal items inside the hut.

The 92nd were due to have their passing-out parade when they completed their own training at Easter 1962. The sight of the trophy mine outside their huts was galling and McKenna devised an ambitious plan to get it back. There were four elements to the plan. First, in the middle of the night before the 92nd's passing out parade a small group would creep across the large grassed area known as the Arena which separated the 94th from the 92nd and detach the mine from its booby-traps. This involved cutting the ropes attached to the mine and fastening the ends to the sides of the huts so that the items inside the hut would not fall noisily to the floor.

Secondly, a trolley would be used to transport the mine as quietly as possible to a hiding place within the 94th's hutments. Thirdly, 'A' Squadron's junior entries, the 97th and the 100th, would get dressed in combat fatigues and place themselves amongst building works adjacent to the Arena to fight off the 92nd if they woke up and pursued the mine. Finally, a group of us (me included) would be dressed in modified uniforms to pretend to be RAF police in the event of a mass brawl and would then order everyone to return to their huts whilst taking charge of the mine.

The plan worked like a dream. I can still recall the ghostly sight of the mine on its trolley gliding noiselessly in the starlight towards its destination – there was no need for the mass brawl or the police intervention. I enormously enjoyed watching the 92nd emerging the next morning in their spotless passing-out uniforms to stare in consternation at the empty space where their precious trophy had been the night before!

I didn't always see eye to eye with McKenna. One particular event resulted in a serious rift. Every year there was a prestigious inter-entry drill competition which took place on the parade ground with the whole camp watching. When it was the turn of the 94th Entry to take part I was determined that we should win. That was a huge ask. Being a small entry of some 70 individuals we needed nearly everyone to volunteer in order to whittle the participants down to just under 50 of the most accomplished for the squad itself.

McKenna and a group of colleagues who were

becoming increasingly detached from the more military aspects of air force life made it clear that they would not volunteer and indeed pointedly mocked our drill squad whilst we were training on the parade ground in preparation for the competition.

For the competition we needed firstly to achieve perfect co-ordination of the drill movements, marching without orders for several minutes and carrying out a succession of moves including funeral drill, rotating our rifles so that the assessor could look from the side of the squad and see all three ranks rotating their rifles in perfect synchronisation. This required endless practice.

Secondly, our kit needed to be cleaned and polished faultlessly ready for the inspection at the start of the drill sequence. The 94th's huts during the weeks before the competition had items of kit and rifles hanging from the rafters – bayonets painted and polished, rifles varnished, webbing scrubbed clean of the usual RAF blue-grey and blancoed white – boots bulled (spit and polished) till they reflected like mirrors.

On top of this there were 'tricks of the trade' for the day itself. Immediately before the initial inspection of the squad there was a 'present arms' – a three-part move involving bringing the rifle in front of you, hitting the magazine of the rifle with the flat of your left hand and slamming the heel of your right foot onto the ground behind you. To make the maximum impact we loosened the metal heel-cap of the right boot by unscrewing it slightly. We also left the magazine of the rifle slightly loose. Thus, when the order came to present arms the effect was dramatic. As we silently counted 'one left right, two left right three' the actual moves were punctuated by loud bangs as the magazines clicked into position on 'two' and the heels hit the ground on 'three'.

We drilled relentlessly for weeks – all in our own time after the normal day's education and training had finished. Everything depended on our turn-out and performance on the big day. We gave it everything. Not only did we win – we won with the highest score ever achieved at RAF Locking.

I was ecstatic. Immediately afterwards the Flight Lieutenant in overall charge of our entry came to our huts similarly elated. He said "That was amazing –I've arranged for you all to have a 36-hour pass to leave the camp". I said "Who do you mean?" He said "Well, the whole entry". I said "I don't think that's fair – I think it should only be for those who volunteered for the drill squad. There were others who mocked us from the sidelines throughout our training". He said "Well, I'm disappointed in you Parker – you have been the strongest advocate of entry spirit and solidarity." Nevertheless, with the strong support of the rest of the drill squad the 36-hour pass ended up being restricted to the volunteers.

However, McKenna had the last laugh. He quickly arranged for an old friend from Manchester to send him a letter claiming that his father had died and that the funeral would take place on the weekend of the 36-hour pass. McKenna was then granted a 48-hour pass! Needless to say, his father continued to thrive for a great many years following his reported sad demise.

Because he subsequently played a huge role in my

later life I need to say more about Mike McKenna. His mum was a hard-working and religious woman. She worked at Gallagher's cigarette factory, near Middleton. The family lived in a council house on the Langley Estate. McKenna's dad, as far as I could make out, had never done a day's work in his life, and during the war he was a conscientious objector, which meant he hadn't been in the armed forces.

He was, however, extremely well-read. He enjoyed reading philosophy and he passed this onto Mike, his only son, from a very young age. When Mike was about six or seven his mum, who was a committed Catholic, was telling him that he should believe in God but his dad was getting him to read the agnostic philosopher Bertrand Russell and saying, "You see Mike, there's no proof there is a God, so there probably isn't one." So, at six or seven, Mike was reading Bertrand Russell which, significantly, fed later into his sharing Russell's opposition to nuclear weapons.

Before he joined up Mike had got a motorbike on hire purchase but fairly soon smashed it up. He still had to pay it off. He had to get money from somewhere and decided to join the RAF, even though that meant signing on until he was thirty.

Both of us were allocated to the technical specialism known as Air Radio Bomber. We trained on several radio and radar systems but the main focus was on the equipment in the V-Bombers - the Victors, Valiants and Vulcans which comprised the nation's nuclear bomber force.
We could hardly have been destined for a more vital

area of the country's armed forces. These aircraft were kept in a state of permanent readiness to hit Russia with nuclear weapons as part of the deterrence strategy known as Mutually Assured Destruction. We were in the depths of the Cold War. The West, organised within NATO and led by the United States, confronted the Communist bloc, organised within the Warsaw Pact and led by the Soviet Union. Both sides maintained a huge stockpile of nuclear weapons sufficient to wipe out life on earth several times over with a view to deterring the other side from ever attacking.

As indicated earlier, I was intensely patriotic, fiercely loyal to the RAF and fully supportive of the role it was playing in national defence. However, during our final year of training I became aware that McKenna was developing a very different outlook.

The Campaign for Nuclear Disarmament (CND) had been in the headlines for several years, making clear its opposition to Britain's possession of nuclear weapons by holding marches and organising publicity stunts. The philosopher Bertrand Russell, whose writings were familiar to McKenna, was jailed for seven days in September 1961 for 'breach of the peace' after taking part in an anti-nuclear demonstration in London. The magistrate offered to exempt him from jail if he pledged himself to 'good behaviour' which the 89-year old Russell refused to do, upon which he was transferred to Brixton Prison.

McKenna gradually became more and more drawn to CND, together with a group of his friends within the 94th Entry. They started going on CND demonstrations and coming back with all kinds of anti-nuclear literature. I became more and more angry, arguing "Look, we're here to defend this country and it requires nuclear weapons!"

These arguments became so bitter that during our final year in 1962 there were two clearly opposed factions within the entry with myself increasingly taking on the role of leading the opposition to McKenna. It proved to be a losing battle. I was finally worn down by the argument that as there was a balance of terror between the two major political blocs the UK didn't need to have its own nuclear arsenal because America and Russia with their huge preponderance of weapons could maintain deterrence on their own.

The case was that if Britain could justify having its own nuclear weapons it wouldn't be long before many other countries would acquire them – a process known as 'the proliferation of nuclear weapons'. And deterrence would break down because if missiles could come from anywhere you wouldn't know who to hit in retaliation. The development of submarine-based missiles tended to lend credibility to this analysis.

During the Autumn of 1962 the global political climate suddenly worsened dramatically. It was the time of the Cuban Missile Crisis, arguably the closest the world had ever come to nuclear war. American spy planes had spotted nuclear missiles and launch sites on Cuba, 90 miles from the USA. Soviet ships were then seen carrying further missiles on their way to Cuba and on 22nd October President Kennedy ordered a naval blockade to stop the ships. He also demanded the removal of the missiles already there. After thirteen tense days, a naval stand-off and lots of top-secret negotiations, the Soviet Union agreed to remove the missiles. However, many people felt that nuclear war had been imminent.

Members of the 94th Entry at Locking were getting in cars and going to Weston Super Mare to have a final drink before the world ended. It later emerged that a bomber pilot from RAF Coningsby had told his wife to get in the car and go to Scotland, as far away as she could from London, because he was about to fly a nuclear bomber to Russia, and there was no way he was going to get back and England would be destroyed.

It was about that time that I decided that I needed to support CND. I went home to Folkestone for Christmas 1962 to see my mum and stepfather. I remember saying to them, "I'm not sure I'm going to be in the air force for much longer because I don't think we should have these nuclear weapons."

By a fateful coincidence, McKenna and I were both held back for a further month to re-take a technical test when our three-year course at Locking finished in December 1962. When we returned to Locking in January, McKenna asked if I would jointly sign a letter with him to the pacifist newspaper 'Peace News' setting out our views. I agreed, starting a chain of events which was to change my life.

Our letter, referring to a soldier who was being court martialled for anti-nuclear activities, read:

A forces CND group?

We find it extremely encouraging to read of further dissent within the forces. We are sure there are many more who, after having enlisted, have found that their political and moral convictions have radically altered.

It occurred to us that many such people, either pacifists or merely nuclear unilateralists, could have considerable success in propagating their ideas in the close communities peculiar to service life; but, lacking support of either a moral or practical nature, they are loath to try. From our own experience we have found that such activities can yield considerable success, and wondered if it would be possible to provide the above-mentioned support and to co-ordinate activities and ideas by forming a services CND group.

Would anyone interested in such a project, either within the forces or outside, please contact us.

686334 J/T Parker, E. R.,
686330 J/T McKenna, M.,
Bk J.3, c/o Station P.O.,
RAF, Locking,
Weston-super-Mare,
Somerset.

Credit: Peace News 1 February, 1963

Peace News was published every Friday. We were caught off-guard therefore when, just as we were finishing our final workshop test on a Thursday afternoon, we were summoned to the office of the Camp Commandant – somewhere we'd never been before.

It was located in a large hut. At the far end of the room the Wing Commander in charge of the entire camp was sitting behind his desk with his adjutant standing beside him. He read out an article from the Guardian newspaper referring to a letter due to appear in Peace News the following day. He said "Is this you?" Obviously, it was. The Commandant then said, "Right, there are a group of press people outside the gates wanting to interview you. Are you prepared to see them?" which, come to think of it, was very good of him.

I stood rigidly to attention and said, "Yes, Sir." McKenna said, "No" but then changed his mind. We were on the front pages the next day. My mum always got a copy of the Daily Mail and there was a CND sign at the top of the page with a headline reading 'Ban the Bomb Cell in Top-Secret RAF Camp.' She started reading, thinking, "Oh Ed will be interested in this," and then suddenly realised it was about me and, allegedly, her hair turned grey overnight!

After that, things happened quickly. We were moved immediately into the cells in the guardroom, adjacent to the camp's main gate. We were treated very politely by the guards though the accommodation was understandably spartan, with wooden benches for beds. We were interviewed separately by the RAF's Special Investigation Branch (SIB) who I think did their job superbly. There were two of them, dressed in civilian clothes and whilst one stood to the side taking notes, the other one invited me to sit down and started chatting about incidental matters such as the quality of the camp's food before casually remarking "Oh, and this ban the bomb stuff – how did you get involved in that?"

McKenna, citing previous experience with the police, had advised me to say nothing. However, I found myself explaining my newly acquired thinking and, although this then became a statement presented as part of the prosecution's evidence I was glad to be able to get it on the record. A court-martial was convened with the charge against us that we had acted 'contrary to Section 69 of the Air Force Act' which required 'good order and Air Force discipline' in that we had 'caused the following

Credit: Peace News 22 February, 1963

words to be published in a publication know as Peace News' – and then the wording of our letter.

I later found out that the Special Investigation Branch had been active in following up members of the 94th in

32

the places they'd been posted to after leaving Locking. Flash Garratt, who had popped back and visited me in Locking just before my arrest, has given me a graphic account of his interview with the SIB in which they quizzed him on what he knew of my and McKenna's views and whether he would be prepared to work with nuclear weapons – to which he replied with something less than total enthusiasm in view of their destructive potential but said that as a ground radar specialist he didn't think it was likely to happen!

Allan Thomas was also interviewed. By coincidence this happened a few days after he had lost his wallet. He confused his interrogator by replying to the opening question "You know what this is about, don't you?" by replying "Yes, have you found it?" Allan was interviewed at the same time as Alan 'Chippy' Wood who was an outspoken supporter of nuclear disarmament. They were both engaged in highly sensitive work at the same location and Chippy was subsequently transferred to a different role elsewhere.

McKenna and I were referred to solicitors in Weston-Super-Mare to prepare our defence and they to their credit engaged a first-class Queen's Counsel (QC) from London who, at the hearing, spoke so eloquently on our behalf that I thought we might receive a medal rather than a custodial sentence! However, this was not to be. Very quickly the verdict came back: 'Eight months in custody and discharged with ignominy from the RAF'. As we were marched away under escort I kept thinking "Oh, no – eight months". Behind me I could hear McKenna whispering excitedly "We've been discharged!"

Back we went to the guardroom. A number of humorous episodes then ensued. The Committee of 100, a militant subset of CND, was maintaining a continuous picket in our support just outside the camp gates. I had taken to standing on my wooden bed looking out between the bars of the cell window simply to see the daylight. Suddenly the door of the cell burst open and one of the guards turned to the sergeant accompanying him and said "There you are, Sarge – he's signaling to them!" Since there was no way the demonstrators could be seen from my cell window I escaped retribution.

On another occasion, McKenna and I were out of our cells in the main office of the guardroom together with the sergeant in charge. The sergeant turned to me and said "I suppose we'd better make an inventory of your kit before you go off to prison". The two of us then went to my cell and I thoughtlessly pulled the door shut behind me, locking us both in. "Oh no" said the sergeant – "how are we going to get out?" The only way was to call loudly for McKenna and then to tell him, through the spyhole in the cell door, how to find the keys in the main office and release us. He found this extremely amusing though I suspect that the sergeant had seldom been more worried.

Less amusing was a conversation with another inmate. He had had previous convictions and had spent time in the detention barracks at Colchester in Essex. "What was it like?" I asked. He described a gruelling regime. Up at 5.30am dressed for inspection followed by an assault course and another inspection. If any faults were found on this inspection, punishment drill at the double – and on it went.

"Good heavens" I said – "I don't think I could stand that – what if you just refuse to do it?" Then you get put in Specials" he said. "What's Specials?" I asked. He then described something so horrific that I could hardly believe it. "You're put in a straitjacket with a metal rod down the back which is pure agony – then you're put into a sealed box the size of an oven. After 24 hours no-one ever refuses to do as they're told". Sceptical though I may have been about this, it was later confirmed in a BBC-TV series called 'Man Alive'.

He then said "Of course, that's if you're lucky". "What if you're not lucky?" I asked with some trepidation. "If you're not lucky" he said, "You get sent to Shepton Mallet". "And what happens at Shepton Mallet?" I asked. "Shepton Mallet" he said – there was a long pause – "People have been sent to Shepton Mallet and never heard of again".

A few days later McKenna and I stood before the desk of one of the admin officers. "Tomorrow", he said "you will be transferred to Her Majesty's Prison & Detention Barracks, Shepton Mallet".

Chapter 3

Shepton Mallet Prison

The winter of 1962-63 was the coldest of the century, with blizzards, snow drifts, frozen pipes in houses, people skating on rivers, and temperatures lower than -20 °C. It was so cold that the sea froze for a mile off Herne Bay in Kent, snow lay 20 feet deep on Exmoor and 6 feet deep in Manchester. Icebergs floated into the Mersey.

At the end of February 1963 McKenna and I were transferred from RAF Locking to Her Majesty's Prison and Detention Barracks, Shepton Mallet. We travelled

Sentences confirmed

Michael McKenna (left) of Middleton, Manchester, and Edward Parker (right) of Cheriton, Folkestone, the two airmen who were sentenced to eight months' imprisonment on February 22 for writing to " Peace News " suggesting the formation of a CND group in the forces. The sentences have now been confirmed, an Air Ministry spokesman told " Peace News " last Monday, and the two men will be serving their sentence at the military prison at Shepton Mallet, Somerset.

Credit: Peace News 8 March, 1963

in the back of an RAF car with two military policemen in the front. As we passed through the Somerset countryside we looked out at snow-covered fields, sparkling in the afternoon sun, and I jokingly said to McKenna, "It's a good job we weren't sent here a couple of months ago or we'd have been breaking up ice in the prison yard." Next day that's exactly what we were doing.

Michael Portillo has made an excellent TV programme on Shepton Mallet Prison as part of his 'Hidden History of Britain' series. It shows just how grim the place was. It was built in 1610, in the reign of King James I and during Shakespeare's lifetime. It was known as a tough prison even before the military took over in 1939. Reggie and Ronald Kray served time there in the early 1950's during their national service. There was a double gallows, last used in 1945 and removed in 1967 – four years after I arrived.

Having heard about the prison previously I thought I was ready for what lay in store but our reception shook me. Our car turned abruptly from the main road into a narrow alleyway, on either side of which were huge stone walls blocking out the daylight. It was oppressive even before we got into the building. The car emerged into a town square and stopped in front of a large prison door. One of the RAF police banged loudly and a smaller door set into it swung open and the intimidation began immediately.

The place was run by the army and our designation changed abruptly from the RAF rank of 'Junior Technician' to 'Soldier Under Sentence (SUS)'. We had to stand to attention addressing the prison guards as 'Staff' whilst they shouted into our faces.

We were marched into separate 'holding' cells where guards continued to scream at us through the spyholes. We were then brought before the prison's Block Commandant who said "Your fame has preceded you. If you talk about politics you will find yourself in Specials".

Next we were marched off to our separate cells. The prison layout was similar to other prisons, familiar from films and TV. Long balconies were located around a central hall, with rows of cells set back from the edge of the landing. Each level had wire netting stretched between the balconies across the central area. Apparently this had been installed at Shepton following a prison riot a few years previously as a precaution against prison staff being thrown over the balconies.

The cells were small, single occupancy, with just enough room for an iron bed and a locker and the stone floors were very highly polished. The boots of the inmates never touched the floor. Instead, everyone stood on floorpads and continually 'skated' back and forth in order to keep the floors ready for instant inspection. Similarly, no-one ever slept in the sheets provided but instead used blankets so that the bedpack, including the sheets, could be left largely made up ready for inspection at any time. There were no wash basins or toilets in the cells – chamber pots were provided.

Orders were given by means of a whistle. Cells were unlocked before meals or activities but no-one could come out before a whistle was blown. Inmates then stood outside their cells. Another blast on the whistle meant turn to face the end of the landing. A final blast meant march off to whatever came next.

My first contact with a fellow inmate occurred soon after my arrival when the cells were unlocked prior to the 5pm evening meal. My cell was on the ground floor. As I looked past the partly open door to the cell opposite the guy inside peered back and whispered "Have you got any ticker?" I signalled back that I didn't understand. Soon afterwards I found out that 'ticker' was a much-valued commodity - partially burnt rag used to light cigarettes.

I didn't smoke which was a blessing because those who did seemed preoccupied with a craving for cigarettes. We received a weekly allowance of two shillings and sixpence (twelve and a half pence in decimal currency) to be spent in the prison shop. For those who smoked the purchases were invariably tobacco, cigarette papers and a flint to light the ticker. The flint could be struck with a fragment of razor blade to create a spark which in turn would cause the ticker to catch and glow. As I didn't smoke I could spend my allowance on luxuries such as sugar and sweets!

The daily routine began when a hand-bell was rung at 5.30am. Prisoners had to get their feet on the floor immediately and as they got dressed the doors were unlocked and the inmates assembled outside with their chamber pots. On the whistle they marched off to empty the pots down one of the two toilets on each landing before swilling them down at nearby sinks. After returning to the cells they re-emerged with drinking mugs and collected a mug-full of hot water and their own numbered razor before going back to the cells to shave. A final trip to the sinks took place to return the razor and have a quick splash of water before getting back to the cells for kit inspection.

Breakfast was the best meal of the day – at all other times I was ravenous. At breakfast time we queued up for a bowl of porridge (inevitably!), a plate with some tomato, a slice of bacon – or, on alternate days, a sausage – and two pieces of toast. We also had a mug of tea. We were locked in our cells to eat breakfast and enjoyed some peace and quiet until about 9.30am when we were let out to go to work. The day ended with our being locked back into our cells at 7.30pm with lights being turned out at 8.30pm.

On our first full day McKenna and I were, indeed, set to work breaking ice in the prison yard, just as I'd joked in the car the day before. Whoever had arranged for the clearing of the snow in the prison yard had got it piled up on the side that never got any sun. It was rock-solid and took some breaking up with pickaxes.

Once the prison yard was cleared we were transferred to a work regime called Camp Repair which was basically something to keep you busy until they sorted out some other work for you to do. Camp Repair was essentially a long row of people doing pointless things. One activity was sandpapering a bucket. After an hour you'd be required to give the bucket to the next person who would then sandpaper it for a further hour whilst you were given a chair to sandpaper for an hour before passing it on to the next person. This went until the next meal break, lunch or tea. Meals were taken communally on trestle tables set up in the prison block.

There were ten prison rules listed on notices posted up in various locations. During his first morning on Camp Repair McKenna started humming a tune. Within moments one of the guards said "Go sick, McKenna!" That was when we found out that "Go sick" meant "See a doctor who will confirm that you're fit to undergo punishment" and that meant you were on a charge for an offence of some kind. The charge that McKenna was on was 'unnecessary whistling or singing'. You could be put in Specials – or lose remission - for a breach of prison rules. We got to know that in Shepton Mallet, unlike Colchester, Specials involved solitary confinement and a diet of bread and water. McKenna was just given a warning.

A few days later I found myself on a charge. After my morning shave I returned from putting my razor back to find in my cell a particularly unpleasant guard called Staff Sergeant Maggs. He said "Look at the state of this cell, I've never seen such a mess". I was nonplussed. The kit on my bed was perfectly laid out apart from a towel I'd left on it following my shave. He then called in another guard and said "Look at the state of this man's cell". "It's a disgrace" said his colleague, "I've never seen anything like it". "Go sick, Parker" said Maggs. Thus I found myself charged with being 'idle, negligent and careless'.

After a few derisory moments with the prison doctor I was brought before the Commandant of the prison block. Maggs began by stating "I entered the accused's cell and found it in a state of complete disorder. No attempt had been made to get it ready for inspection". His colleague confirmed Maggs' baseless accusations. When it was my turn to make a statement I said "What you have heard is a total fabrication". I then went on to describe in detail the way my kit had been laid out. It was clear from the Commandant's expression that he found my account more convincing than Maggs' but he nevertheless said "There is no need for the Staff Sergeant to have lied" and went on "If there is any repetition you will be sent to Specials but on this occasion I will merely admonish (warn) you".

This was not the only occasion on which I suffered from Maggs' disfavour. He seemed to pick on me because he particularly disliked my views. However, I never ended up in Specials despite Maggs' best efforts.

Before long I progressed from Camp Repair to something called Bed Shops. I actually enjoyed that. Bed Shops received old mattresses from throughout the army. Prison inmates would cut the mattresses open at one end and pull out the stuffing which proved to be horsehair for officers and coir for other ranks. My job was to put this material through a machine which tore it apart so that it could be put back into the mattress, sown back up and sent out to where it had come from – good as new!

I worked the machine in a small well-ventilated hut with a colleague from the Royal Ulster Rifles. We got on really well with lots of banter. However, it was my first experience of the Northern Irish sectarianism which came into such prominence a few years later. Needless to say, my colleague was a committed Protestant with attitudes to Catholics which I had happily never encountered, didn't like to hear and could never understand.

After a month in Shepton you were allowed to receive a visit. I looked forward to this enormously and on the appointed day was shown into a large, bleak reception hall in the middle of which, crouched round a small table, were my mother and stepfather. They looked pretty glum, as well they might, having entered such a forbidding institution, but as I looked so elated at seeing them they soon cheered up and my mum said how glad she was to see me looking so well in contrast to her worst fears.

After a few more weeks McKenna and I unexpectedly got some amazing and very welcome news. One of the few pleasant moments in the prison week was when we queued up to spend our allowance in the prison shop. The guard in charge was a friendly and helpful individual. When he saw my name he said "Oh, Parker – you're one of those getting early release". I was astonished "No, Staff" I said "I'm Parker". "Yes, that's right" he said "You and McKenna".

The next moment the tannoy came to life "Soldiers Under Sentence Parker and McKenna to report to the Commandant's Office immediately". At that very moment McKenna appeared. "Mike" I said "we're being released early". He laughed this off until I made clear that I was absolutely serious. Off we went and the Commandant read out that as a result of an Air Ministry review our sentence had been changed from "eight months imprisonment and discharge with ignominy" to "four months detention and discharge under administrative arrangements – services no longer required".

A few weeks later I received a letter from the House of Commons. It was from Brian Walden, a Labour MP for a Birmingham constituency. In it he explained that it was he who had raised our case in Parliament. He said that although he did not agree with our views he felt that eight months was a disproportionate sentence for having written a letter to a newspaper. He later became a highly respected TV personality, conducting in-depth interviews with leading politicians of the day. He will forever have my gratitude for taking up our case unprompted and getting a reduction in our sentence. Sadly he died in May 2019 at the age of 86.

With the change in our sentence from 'imprisonment' to 'detention' we had to move from the prison block ('A' Block) to the adjacent detention block ('B' Block). The regime in 'B' Block turned out to be significantly less oppressive than in 'A' Block. The cells had been knocked through to accommodate four prisoners in two pairs of bunk beds. The chance to talk to others about their experiences made all the difference in passing the time.

There was 'Barry the Gnome', who had deserted from the army to become a beatnik, roaming the islands of the Mediterranean. There was a Scottish guardsman who was serving two years for assault but was desperate to be re-enlisted in the army and spent most of his time writing letters of appeal. Finally, there was an engaging

Liverpudlian from the Liverpool Tank Corps, one of many from his unit sentenced to a term in Shepton following a mass brawl with German civilians in Berlin. They were recognisable throughout the prison by the silver tank insignia on their black berets. One was the camp barber, a tall, muscular individual who used a cut-throat razor which put me in fear of my life whenever it was my turn for a hair-cut!

One example of the more relaxed regime in 'B' Block was the distribution, during the Saturday lunch period, of incoming mail with the names of the recipients being called out by the guards to various humorous and ribald responses from the assembled masses. This reached unprecedented levels with me and McKenna. We began to receive huge numbers of letters, clearly orchestrated by CND, addressed to Prisoner of Conscience Parker or McKenna. As letter followed letter with the guards calling out our names together with the "Prisoner of Conscience" designation other inmates would be shouting out such things as "Where can we join – we'd like a letter too".

When we got out I vowed that I would never do anything which might get me sent back to prison – a vow I'm not sure I completely kept as later events will demonstrate though I never did serve any more time in prison. I am nevertheless glad to have gone through the experience. Loss of freedom is sadly not the worst thing people can suffer in today's horrific world. However, it is something many people endure and I am glad to have some understanding of their situation.

We were released on the morning of Friday 12th April

1963 to a further strange sequence of events. There was sizeable group of demonstrators outside supporting our actions together with a number of reporters. Also released with us by chance was a sailor who had shared McKenna's cell. The reporters were keen to find out whether McKenna and I had changed our views during our imprisonment. Being disabused of this they turned to the sailor – to find out that, no doubt under McKenna's influence, he too professed a firm commitment to unilateral nuclear disarmament.

Our small procession then made its way through the streets of Shepton to, for some reason, the local war memorial. Among the 33 servicemen listed there as having died in the Second World War was one named E.R Maggs.

There was a postscript to all this. RAF Marham was – and still is - an important airbase in Norfolk. In the 1960's it was home not only to RAF V-bombers but also to elements of the US Air Force guarding the nuclear weapons. As such the base became a target in May 1963 for large CND anti-nuclear demonstrations with demonstrators attempting to break through the boundary fences. The RAF personnel at Marham were deployed in the unfamiliar task of repelling the demonstrators.

Several of the RAF personnel involved happened to be recent arrivals from the 94th Entry of which I and McKenna had been part. Pete Purdy, Ewan Tennant and Colin Clayton were astonished to see large pictures of me and McKenna on the banners being held aloft by the demonstrators as martyrs to their cause.

Leave ended up being cancelled for the four consecutive weekends on which the demonstrations took place. Ewan Tennant was particularly upset at not being able to get back for a month to see his girlfriend in Weston-Super-Mare. Colin Clayton had a memory of a demonstrator who got through the fence and started venting his anger at a Bloodhound surface-to-air missile, presumably mistaking it for a nuclear Inter Continental Ballistic Missile (ICBM). Pete Purdy was even featured on the front page of Peace News apprehending a female demonstrator.

When they were not repelling CND demonstrators the ex-94th personnel were spending a week at a time stuck in a compound at the end of the Marham runway on Quick Reaction Alert (QRA) duties so that the V-bombers could be airborne within the four-minute warning of nuclear attack. Such were the 1960's!

Chapter 4

Working with CND

As I stood outside Shepton Mallet Prison following my
release I realised I didn't know what I was going to do
next. Until then I had been fed, clothed and housed
without being required to do very much on my own
initiative. Perhaps the high incidence of re-offending
was partly because other prisoners had the same
anxiety about managing on their own?

The first thing that happened after our procession to
the Shepton Mallet war memorial was that McKenna
and I were invited to lunch at the home of the CND
organiser from Banwell near RAF Locking with whom
we had been in close touch in the weeks before we wrote
our fateful letter. We were happy to dine on the fish and
chips he proudly offered us, convinced as he was that
our prison diet would have been far inferior. In fact we
always had fish and chips as a special treat on Fridays
in Shepton but we didn't tell him!

Sometime after this McKenna and I found ourselves in
the offices of Peace News in London being interviewed
about our experiences by the newspaper's editor, Hugh
Brock. After the interview, as I recall, we had nowhere
to stay and ended up sleeping on the office floor till the
next morning.

Following this we were approached by a CND activist,
George Clark, who was in the final stages of putting

together a project called 'Campaign Caravan Workshops' which involved equipping a 'battle bus' with typewriters, a duplicator, a loudhailer and a team of volunteers to spread the word about nuclear disarmament.

The idea was to go to different areas, beginning in the forthcoming summer holiday period when university students would be available, to try to set up CND branches. The first target was to be a rural area. Yes, you've guessed it – Shepton Mallet! Next would be a suburban area – Welwyn Garden City – and finally, an industrial area – the Glasgow shipyards as I recall.

McKenna and I were happy to join in and the bus duly made its way down to Somerset. We had negotiated with a farmer to park the bus and camp in his field.

Our daily routine was to set off after breakfast for one of the Somerset villages whilst perusing the morning papers for topical stories we could weave into a leaflet, which would be typed up and duplicated during the journey. Earlier, we would have identified a meeting place, usually a church hall loaned by a sympathetic vicar or priest, for an evening meeting which would be publicised in the leaflet.

One of our number, a certain Paul Fluckiger, was always keen to be first on the loudhailer. As the bus pulled into its parking space he would get out and bellow "Radiation is making YOU sterile – come to a meeting tonight to set up a Frome (or wherever) branch of the Campaign for Nuclear Disarmament". The rest of us would hand out leaflets in the street then spend the rest of the day going door to door with leaflets and clipboards, noting down the details of anyone who proved sympathetic to be used once a branch was set up.

This all seemed to go remarkably well. There were very strong feelings about CND at the time – for and against – but we always survived the doorstep encounters and ended up with enough people at the meetings to get things going.

From time to time the bus would make a long journey to a farm in Warwickshire owned by someone who turned out to be funding the operation – a millionaire named Howard Cheney. This was the project's base camp and during our visits there would be folk singing round a campfire and eloquent contributions from academics and activists. It was all very inspiring.

On our final visit, as the 'rural' project came to an end, it was suggested that I should remain at the farm when the bus, with a slightly different team, went on to Welwyn Garden City. I've never been quite sure how this happened – the unlikely rationale was that I could help service the bus when it came back – but, in any event, there then followed a bizarre series of episodes during the remainder of the summer and early autumn.

Cheney's farm was in a remote location near a place called Upper Brailes, a few miles from the village of Shipston-on-Stour. Howard Cheney's fortune was derived from the family's ownership of. C.W.Cheney & Son, a highly successful Birmingham company specialising in the manufacture of locks for luggage and other kinds of cases. He seems to have been a very benevolent employer. However, during my time on his farm I found him to be somewhat eccentric. He later achieved some notoriety by refusing to pay the proportion of taxes going towards armaments and barricading the farm against officials attempting to enforce payment.

The farm was fairly large but didn't seem to produce anything, though Cheney kept bees and his daily routine was to wander round after breakfast tending the bees in appropriate protective clothing. I was allocated a disused cottage opposite the Cheney family's farmhouse. The cottage was sparsely furnished with little to commend it other than cold running water and a bed. It was semi-detached and next door there lived a delightful family named Williams.

Cheney seemed to have a strong work ethic – at least for other people. As I had no clear role at the farm he soon became very agitated by what he saw as my indolence and set me to work 'spudding thistles' which I recall as wandering the vast acreage with a hoe looking for thistles and other weeds to dig up and put in a bag for disposal. When the Williams family returned in the evening after a day's work elsewhere they would start work in their cottage garden, apparently to keep in Cheney's good books.

After a week or two Cheney said I should get a job and I ended up doing a bread delivery round for Pargetter's Patisserie of 2, Bridge Street, Stratford-upon-Avon. I loved it - the Pargetter brothers were wonderful to work with and I got to visit all kinds of superb venues – pubs, stately homes etc – when delivering their newly-baked bread and delicious pies. One place I delivered to was the Royal Shakespeare Theatre which had a daily order for bread rolls. I soon realized that these rolls were immediately broken up and thrown into the adjacent River Avon to attract the swans and thus provide an ideal photo-opportunity for the tourists!

Getting to Stratford from the farm was a bit of a problem. It was several miles to the village of Shipston-on-Stour, then 12 miles up the A429 to Stratford. However, this difficulty was soon overcome by the redoubtable Mr. Williams from the cottage next door. He was a milk delivery roundsman for Shipston and was able to give me a lift into the village.

Unfortunately, I hadn't thought to invest in an alarm clock and Mr. Williams needed to start work extremely early and couldn't afford to wait if I was late to meet him outside the cottage. Between us we developed an imaginative solution. We rigged up a piece of rope between our cottages, running from my bedroom to his kitchen. My end was tied round a large piece of metal suspended over an equally large piece of iron plate. His end was tied round the leg of his kitchen table. The first thing Mr. Williams would do when he got up was to untie his end of the rope. This would result in an unearthly clatter in my bedroom as the metal weight fell down. I would wake up with a shock. In fact, before long I would wake up beforehand and stare with trepidation at the weight, waiting in dread for it to come crashing down.

At this point I needed to move very fast in order to get my lift in the milk van. I would race downstairs for a quick splash in some cold water, then run down the path towards the van. At the same time Mr. Williams would emerge from his front door, running with equal determination down his own parallel path.

If I made it in time I would collapse breathlessly into the passenger seat until ejected at the main road in Shipston whereupon I would hitch a lift to Stratford, easy to do in those days. Coming back in the evening was the reverse, though I would usually have to walk from Shipston to the farm. After that it was time for a meal – usually a pie I'd brought back from work – then an hour or two pretending to work in the cottage garden alongside the Williams family.

In all the time I was there I was never invited into the Cheney family home – until one evening when Howard Cheney rather grumpily informed me that there was a phone call for me. I went in and was astounded to hear McKenna's voice inviting me to join him for a drink at a pub in nearby Banbury, together with his good friend Morgan O'Brien and O'Brien's brother.

It says much for how I'd been ground down during my rural isolation that I began to say I couldn't get to Banbury and that, in any event, Cheney would disapprove. McKenna's disbelief was enough to change my mind and somehow I found my way to the pub and experienced huge relief at being once again in convivial and cheerful company. McKenna and O'Brien convinced me that it was absurd for me to stay at the farm doing nothing of consequence and the next morning I made my apologies to Cheney, his family, the Williams family and the Pargetter brothers – and began a journey to Manchester for one of the strangest and happiest periods of my life.

Chapter 5

Hulme Hall

I first stumbled across Hulme Hall – or more accurately 43, Hulme Hall Lane, a grim terraced house off the Oldham Road in Manchester – on a bitterly cold and foggy night in December 1962.

It was towards the end of my time in the RAF. Mike McKenna had persuaded me to spend the first few days of our Christmas leave at his parents' home on the Langley Estate in Middleton, Manchester before I left to go on to my own home in Folkestone.

We got off the train late in the evening at Manchester's Piccadilly station to find that thick fog had reduced visibility to a few yards. It was freezing cold. All my prejudices about life being 'tough up north' were confirmed immediately – and reinforced throughout the rest of my stay.

Mike announced that before going to his parents' home he wanted me to meet a friend of his, Morgan O'Brien, who lived nearby. We walked from the station up the busy Oldham Road, the sounds of traffic muffled by the fog. It was nearly half an hour before we turned off at Hulme Hall Lane and made our way to No. 43.

The front door let immediately onto the pavement, exactly as in the TV series Coronation Street, unlike what I was used to in the south. Mike knocked at the door, then, to my astonishment, on receiving no answer he put his shoulder to the door and pushed it open.

Once inside the hall Mike knocked on the first door on the left before walking in. Inside the dingy room was a double bed, covered with coats for warmth as far as I could tell and, as we entered, a figure rose from the bed, dressed in several layers of clothing, and Mike introduced him as his friend, Morgan O'Brien.

Morgan reacted with good humour to this unexpected intrusion. He suggested that we should go through to the lounge. On entering I noticed a large cavity in the wall where the fireplace should have been. On the table were the remains of a large loaf with a breadknife sticking out of it and half an unwrapped pack of margarine alongside.

Morgan was an engaging Irishman in his late twenties with a large red beard. He had adopted an accent which sounded more mid-European than Irish. He made us tea and I was introduced to 'stera' – or sterilized milk, again something common in the north but largely unknown in the south. The advantage of sterilized milk was that it did not need to be refrigerated – just as well because there was no refrigerator in the house – or, indeed any other domestic appliance.

After this unsettling visit we left to find a bus to Mike's parents' house where the water pipes were frozen up and Mike's mum and dad were locked in perpetual argument, the lingering aftermath of Mike's non-working dad having sold for beer money the lounge carpet purchased by Mike's mum who worked long hours at Gallagher's cigarette factory. She only found out about the sale when she saw the carpet rolled up in the window of a local pawn shop labeled 'Bargain of the week' and arrived home to find bare floorboards. I was relieved to get on the train to Folkestone and I expected never to visit Manchester – or Hulme Hall – ever again. How wrong I was!

Within a few weeks of this Christmas encounter, Mike and I were in Shepton Mallet military prison in Somerset, serving our sentences for publicising our support for the Campaign for Nuclear Disarmament whilst still being members of the Royal Air Force.

Whilst in prison we met another airman. He rejoiced in the name of Paul Carlton Temple and, indeed, appeared to have modeled himself on the fictional detective Paul Temple who was hugely popular at the time as the hero of a weekly radio series.

Our 'Temple' had a handlebar moustache and spoke with an impeccable upper class accent. On his first morning in prison he lined up alongside me on the morning parade inside our cell block. There was a rule of silence during these parades which I observed meticulously, not wishing to lose remission by falling foul of the prison's harsh regime. Temple, however, felt it appropriate to whisper to me, as a fellow airman, an observation regarding the comparative sentences handed out to members of the different armed services.

"I say", he said, "these army types get long sentences, don't they? Some of them are in for months". My response was as brief as I could make it. "Yes".

56

"How long are you in for?" asked Temple. "Eight months" I said. "Oh", said Temple, somewhat downcast. "Dashed shame".

It emerged that Temple was serving 28 days, the minimum sentence which would have landed him in Shepton Mallet. He gave the impression that this was for gun-running in Africa which I accepted at the time, though afterwards concluded that this must have been one of the many flights of fantasy which were fundamental to his personality. 28 days was more likely as a sentence for a less serious offence such as Absence Without Leave (AWOL) for someone they wanted to get rid of anyway.

It later transpired that Temple had nowhere to go at the end of his sentence. McKenna, ever the one to take pity on the dispossessed, decided to refer him to O'Brien's dwelling in Hulme Hall Lane.

Months later, O'Brien told me the tale of Temple's arrival. Another of the many residents of Hulme Hall at the time was Mick McEnery, an old Irishman reminiscent of one of the tramps from a Samuel Beckett novel. McEnery was always dressed in a long brown overcoat and a flat cap. He was never known to take these off. When he went to bed he would pull the cap down over his ears. When he got up he would push the cap back up again.

At the time O'Brien was working as a laboratory assistant at Poundswick Grammar School. He arrived home one day to find McEnery lurking behind a door before stepping out to speak to him in the hushed Irish stage whisper which was his favoured form of address. "There's someone waiting for you upstairs" he said, in tones redolent with mysterious meaning.

"Who?" asked O'Brien. "you'll have to see for yourself", said McEnery. "He insisted on waiting in your room". This was certainly unusual. O'Brien's bedroom was the only reasonably furnished room in the house, kept in this state in unlikely anticipation of the unplanned arrival of female company. The other rooms were mostly in squalid multi-occupation, some with as many as three beds in a room.

O'Brien went into his room to find a stranger there dressed in a silk dinner jacket over his normal clothes. "Ah", said the stranger. "You must be O'Brien. I'm Temple. Take a seat". This in O'Brien's own room!

Too astonished to protest O'Brien did as he was asked. "Have a cigar", said Temple, offering one from a silver cigar case. O'Brien took it and Temple lit it with a stylish lighter.

"Now I'll tell you what we're going to do with this property of yours" he said.

From then on, with the confidence which flowed from the aristocratic background he claimed – completely falsely as it later turned out – Temple assumed a leading role among the extraordinary cast of characters in the Hulme Hall soap opera. Mike McKenna joined these on his own release from prison in April 1963 and I took up residence in September, after the bizarre rural exile on Cheney's farm.

One of those living at Hulme Hall when I arrived was a young lad called Barlow. He was always desperate to get a job but could never hang onto one because he lacked the ability to get out of bed before noon. His excuses for his lateness got ever more ingenious. On one occasion he managed to get a job in a department store. On his first day he arrived late, explaining that as he was leaving the house the front door had fallen off, requiring him to stay at home until it was repaired. On the second day he was even later. His story on this occasion was that, as he was leaving, the landlord fell in the fire requiring Barlow to extinguish the flames, wait for an ambulance and accompany the unfortunate victim to hospital. Unsurprisingly the store decided to dispense with his services before the third day.

The fireplace was in fact an important feature of life at Hulme Hall and the manner of its acquisition occupied a central place in Hulme Hall folklore. I sadly arrived too late to experience the events in person but the tale was repeated so often by the various participants that I felt as though I had been there.

Hulme Hall Lane was in an area of terraced housing where properties were gradually being demolished to make way for the modern estates and tower blocks which became such a despised feature of the 1960s. There was thus a general sense of decay with many houses and shops boarded up and gaps where some had already been demolished.

The impoverished inhabitants of No. 43 eventually realised that as the other properties became vacant they provided a potential source of the good things in life of which they had themselves been unfairly deprived – and their main lack at the time was a fireplace. They devised a scheme whereby when they next saw a house being vacated they would remove its fireplace.

In due course a removal lorry was spotted and, as soon as it departed with the family's possessions, an ill-assorted bunch of miscreants made their way along the road, armed with the pickaxes and crowbars they had painstakingly assembled for the purpose. On entering the property they set about their task with energy and enthusiasm. In no time they had loosened the fireplace and, each carefully grasping a section to ensure that they did not break it, they heaved it away from the wall.

It was at this point that a difficulty emerged. As the workforce gently positioned the fireplace on the floor they saw, through the hole in the wall, that a fire was burning on the other side and that, beyond the fire, a family was staring at them in horrified amazement. As one, the gang realised that their mission had to be aborted and they fled back the way they had come, McEnery complaining loudly that they had left his pickaxe behind.

Despite this misfortune, the experience proved to be of value and, following better reconnaissance, another fireplace was soon acquired. Life at Hulme Hall became somewhat more refined. However, as often happens, what at first appeared as a blessing later revealed itself as a source of some discord.

The problem was the need to obtain fuel. No one could afford to buy coal and so, rather than admitting to being cold and thus being obliged to share in the cost, everyone claimed to be perfectly warm even as the winter weather became ever more bitter. Thus the lounge, by now furnished with several settees acquired from neighbouring empty properties, became occupied by residents dressed in all manner of clothing, often supplemented by whatever bedding they possessed. The tentative enquiry "Are you cold?" would invariably be met by the firmest of denials.

Then, all of a sudden, the collective intelligence of the household alighted on the solution to the problem. All the empty houses contained floorboards! The supply of fuel was thus virtually limitless!

The situation was further improved by the presence during this period of the strongest man to have stayed at Hulme Hall. His name was Bill and he was large and muscular. He had recently been discharged from the army and had walked the many miles from Glasgow to Manchester before coming across Hulme Hall. There was another ex-soldier at Hulme Hall, coincidentally also called Bill, but he was in his seventies and had only one leg, having lost the other in the First World War.

The younger Bill turned out to have the strength to break the floorboards with his bare hands. This enabled the household to stock up with neat piles of fuel and enjoy the most pleasant of temperatures.

There was, though, a problem with breaking up the boards when the younger Bill moved out of Hulme Hall to continue his wanderings. However, a solution was rapidly devised. Whoever was in the front row of the collection of settees would simply position a complete length of floorboard over the back of the settee so that the end of the floorboard was in the fire. In this way a most enjoyable evening could be spent, conversing or reading a book, whilst occasionally pushing the floorboard further into the fire to keep it blazing strongly.

Temple could always be relied on to bring an unexpected frisson to a dull winter's evening. On one such occasion he suddenly suggested to O'Brien and myself that we should go out on the town. With that he put on his bowler hat. O'Brien, not to be outdone, found a deer-stalker hat. Regrettably, I was not able to emulate their sartorial elegance so played a minor role in what followed. On the way out, Temple insisted on taking a rickety kitchen chair. It soon became clear what was in his mind. Hulme Hall Lane was part of the main inner ring road round Manchester and No. 43 was adjacent to the busy Oldham Road. Consequently the heavy ring road traffic had to stop at the Oldham Road traffic lights.

When this happened on this occasion Temple put the chair down on the road facing in the direction of travel and promptly sat down. O'Brien then sat on Temple's knees. As the lights changed they both set off at speed, carrying the chair with them, and running in front of a queue of large lorries angrily hooting in frustration.

After a few hundred yards the pair of them proceeded to the pavement where I joined them. Temple then noticed that a nearby doorway had a sign advertising an Irish club. "Aha" he said, "this will do perfectly". Once through the door we had to go up several flights of stairs.

At the top was a woman behind a table, guarding the nearby door. "We've come for the club" said Temple. Seeing the ill-assorted trio before her the woman began with an unlikely rejoinder. "You can't come in with that chair". "But", replied Temple, his tone one of lofty reproach, "it's a genuine Chippendale – I can't possibly leave it outside". That settled the matter. We had to leave but the evening continued, to the best of my recollection, with great jollity at various pubs and a jazz club. I can't remember where the chair ended up.

This most pleasant way of life could have continued indefinitely but I felt the need to strike out on my own and earn a living. I went for an interview for an electronics job at the Ferranti factory, near Oldham, but the personnel manager pointed out, very reasonably, that having been discharged from the RAF for holding anti-nuclear views it would not be appropriate for me to be employed in a company which held major contracts with the armed forces.

This encounter clarified to me that I was unlikely to get a job in any of the major electronics companies. I then decided that TV repair work offered the best way forward. I got a job at 'Shaw's Rentals' in Reddish Lane, Gorton. The owner, Mr. Shaw, turned out to be an odious, anti-semitic and mean-minded individual who would only pay me £5 a week (£40 in today's money) with the justification that he was doing me a favour as I had no previous experience. I got a room nearby for £3 a week with the result that, surviving on a subsistence diet, I ended up in hospital with malnutrition after a few months. I subsequently got a job as a test engineer at the Radio Rentals factory in Salford which paid much better and gave me a good grounding in TV work.

Meanwhile, both McKenna and O'Brien were planning to leave for London. Whilst in Manchester, McKenna had been studying for 'A' levels at St. John's College of Further Education. He was not earning and both O'Brien and I had been happy to subsidise him during his studies. He had, as far back as his prison days, had a determination to go to university, preferably the London School of Economics (LSE) which he understood to be a hotbed of radical politics. By October 1964 he had achieved this ambition. O'Brien accompanied him to London and began studying 'A' levels himself at Westminster College with similar long-term intentions.

Before going to London, O'Brien had invited Temple to join him in a visit to O'Brien's family home in Ireland. Temple got a job repairing tractor engines at a local garage and stayed there for a year or two. With nothing to keep me in Manchester once McKenna and O'Brien had left I returned to Folkestone where I got a job as an outside TV repair engineer at the local Radio Rentals shop.

Chapter 6

Folkestone feels the 1960's Wind of Change

I returned to Folkestone in summer 1964 and moved back in with my family. I started work at Radio Rentals, a job I enjoyed greatly as it paid well and enabled me to explore the Kent coast and countryside whilst travelling from house to house carrying out domestic TV repairs. The work was made easier because I was already familiar with Radio Rentals TV sets from working with them at the factory in Salford.

Meanwhile I was keen to carry on supporting the Campaign for Nuclear Disarmament and I soon made contact with the local branch organised by David Cowell who became a firm friend and close collaborator. The small but youthful and enthusiastic CND branch met every Wednesday evening in the loft of an old stable in the garden of a florists' shop in Dover Road to plan an imaginative programme of activities.

One ambitious but, in retrospect, utterly absurd idea was to mark out a thirty feet diameter CND sign on a piece of land overlooking the English Channel. The smallest and lightest member of the group, Rodney Mynard, would then be lowered on a rope over the edge of the adjacent cliff with a pot of black paint and a brush.

As the rest of the team walked slowly round above, tracing out the sign, he would be painting it on the iconic White Cliffs of Dover, ideally located to be seen by the ferry-loads of passengers arriving at Folkestone and Dover harbours. It would have made quite an impact but Rodney understandably had second thoughts about his role in this worthy enterprise. To this day David Cowell maintains that the mission was aborted for strategic reasons and not because he was the next smallest and lightest!

We didn't realise it at the time but the man who in 1958 designed the world-famous CND symbol, Gerald Holtom, lived in nearby Hythe and was buried in a local churchyard when he died in 1985.

One thing we did rather more successfully was to organise a march along the cliff-top road from Folkestone to Dover. It poured with rain throughout as I recall. When it ended we held a musical get-together featuring a local folk music trio. They proved to be very entertaining and in conversation afterwards they mentioned that they had been approached by the manager of the prestigious New Metropole Hotel in Folkestone to set up a music appreciation

Credit: Folkestone & Hythe Herald

group, playing records in the hotel's well-appointed art and sculpture gallery.

I said that I'd be pleased to get involved but suggested

that it would be even better to make it a live music event. With that the folk group set up the Folkestone Folk Club which became a roaring success, attracting hundreds of young people every week to the beautiful cliff-top setting enjoyed by the hotel and its channel-facing art gallery. It was there that I met my first wife, Britt, whom I married several years later in 1971.

The folk club also proved to be a suitable venue for spreading the CND message and other radical ideas through the medium of the protest songs which were becoming fashionable throughout the country and, indeed, internationally. I had become a devoted Bob Dylan fan and had previously begun to perform at folk clubs whilst in Manchester – my first attempt was Bob Dylan's 'A hard rain's a-gonna fall' with its anti-war lyrics. At the Folkestone club my repertoire comprised Dylan songs and other pieces popularised by radical folk singers such as Ewan MacColl and Pete and Peggy Seeger.

One minor problem was that both the CND branch meetings and the folk club nights took place every Wednesday evening. I felt I needed to go to both and so turned up fairly late at the folk club, being accused, quite reasonably, of not supporting the earlier acts and trying to steal the show with my last-minute arrival. Despite this, I did manage to see a lot of the other performers, many of whom were absolutely amazing – gypsy-style violinists, blues guitar/harmonica specialists, poets – an unexpected and hugely impressive array of local talent.

A Folkestone musician who didn't frequent the folk club but later became more famous than any of us was

Noel Redding, who became Jimi Hendrix' bass guitarist. He used to spend his time at the Acropolis coffee bar in Folkestone's quaint cobbled High Street which ran steeply down from the town centre to the harbour. A Greek Cypriot, Archie Argiriou, the son of the owner of the Acropolis, became part of the rapidly expanding left-wing crowd with the result that the cafe became our favourite haunt, enhanced by an unbeatable jukebox selection. You could go in at any time, settle into its mock-leather seating and relax to Motown, soul and rhythm'n blues. There was no beating the heady mix of salami rolls and excellent coffee consumed over an hour or two whilst engaging in thought–provoking conversation or gazing at the alabaster mouldings of the Elgin Marbles that adorned one wall. For those who preferred alcohol and harder-edged rock music the coffee bar was opposite the Earl Gray pub and pleasant weekends could be spent gravitating between the two.

Realising that the issue of nuclear weapons could not be dealt with in isolation, the CND group decided that it ought to play an active role in the local Labour Party. A General Election was called for 15th October 1964 and we duly made our presence felt. Folkestone & Hythe had had a Conservative MP ever since it was created as a parliamentary constituency so we felt it was a lost cause. We nevertheless managed to upset the Conservative candidate, the building magnate Albert Costain, by heckling at his public meetings because of his support for white minority rule in Rhodesia.

However, we reserved our main effort for supporting the Labour candidate, David Ennals, in the neighbouring constituency of Dover. In the ensuing election Ennals won the seat from the Conservatives, contributing to Harold Wilson's narrow 4-seat majority.

I fairly soon became disenchanted by Labour's performance in government. I had previously attended an inspiring Harold Wilson rally at Belle Vue, Manchester, which convinced me that radical politics including nuclear disarmament were on the agenda. As this now proved not to be the case I started casting round for alternatives. Central to this quest was the development of a left-wing discussion circle at the large and impressive home of a certain Una Hatfield and her husband.

Mrs. Hatfield was an austere lady of middle years who was very involved with the Communist Party. I was quite drawn to this way of thinking myself, having recently read Dr. Hewlett Johnson's book 'The Socialist Sixth of the World' which led me to believe that the Soviet Union was the land of milk and honey – it took me a year or two to get over this misconception.

A couple of the meetings were attended by a frail little man in a brown pin-striped suit who sat very quietly in the corner. He was Ranjani Palme Dutt, then quite elderly (he was to die in 1974) but still a leading journalist and theoretician in the Communist Party of Great Britain. I don't think we quite realised the significance of the man who sat in our midst.

At the same time I was talking to friends about how there could be social change which might by-pass the established political parties. As well as David Cowell there were, within the Labour Party, friends called Neil

Arding and Alan Bryson who were useful sounding boards. Somehow we developed the notion of 'socialism from below' with the vague idea that trade union-based workplace struggle could challenge the power of those who owned the big industrial enterprises. David and I started leafleting the local Martin Walters Dormobile factory with messages outlining how the creation of surplus value was depriving the workers of their rightful due.

Within the Hatfield discussion circle various older Communist Party figures began to comment, not altogether approvingly, that "these young people are going to give us a revolution". I realized over time that the British Communist Party had a very different perspective called 'The British Road to Socialism' based on reform, not revolution, of which they were suspicious and fearful.

In later years our radical thinking contributed to a couple of unforeseen outcomes – one involved the student activist Tariq Ali and the other was a riot which began in the cobbled High Street – but both of these are best dealt with in a later chapter.

Meanwhile, in early 1965, I received a crucial phone call from Mike McKenna, by then well into his first year at the London School of Economics (LSE). "Can you get up to London?" he said – "I'd really like you to hear a lecture at the university". By chance I was able to take a day off work the following week so I travelled up. It seemed that he wanted me to hear a particular lecturer, Hilde Himmelweit, who had recently written a book called 'Television and the Child'. In any event, whatever Mike's reasons, I was indeed impressed by the lecture. I must have looked a bit odd, sitting in a raked lecture theatre in my working clothes amongst undergraduates who, strange to recall now, were mainly dressed in suits and ties.

The lecturer began by saying "I want to talk about prejudice". I thought – "This is great, I'm very interested in how people can be prejudiced". She went on "Everyone is prejudiced" and I thought "Well, I'm not". She said "Just one word can spark hostility to a whole group of people". Again, I thought "Not me". She said "It could be a word like Tory". With that, I nearly fell off my seat laughing. In those days the word aroused a fiercely adverse reaction in me. Point made.

I thought "If this is what being in university is like it's the life for me – listening to great speakers making excellent jokes!" I turned and whispered to McKenna, "How do I get into a university?" What he told me once more changed my life. He explained that I needed to get 'A' levels. He knew somehow that Wandsworth Technical College had just started an 'A' level course. They would be keen to recruit a cohort of students so I should have no trouble getting enrolled.

He went on to outline a plan for subsequently getting into the London School of Economics. He said I should apply immediately for entry in October 1966 on the standard university application form which had space for first, second and third choices. However, I should take the unusual step of putting down LSE as my only choice. That way, they were likely to grant me an interview as otherwise I would have no chance of a university place.

At interview I should say that I was taking three subjects on a two year 'A' level course but that because of lack of funds I intended to take the exams after one year. They were then likely to specify that I would be admitted if I got acceptable grades in only two subjects. As a fall-back plan, not to be shared with LSE, I should apply separately for a place at Regent Street Polytechnic, which would be likely to accept me with lower grades.

This complicated and ingenious plan worked to perfection, as was so often the case with McKenna's many schemes. LSE agreed to take me onto its B.Sc. Sociology degree course if I got two 'B' grades at 'A' level. Regent Street Polytechnic wanted a 'C' and a 'D' grade. I enrolled at Wandsworth Tech (later South Thames College) in September 1965, moved up to London and got a shared room in Boutflower Road, Clapham Junction – in those days a very rough area but mercifully cheap.

All I now needed to do was to get the required grades in two 'A' level subjects which ended up being in Economics and British Constitution. Since this needed to be achieved within one year, whereas the Wandsworth Tech course was being taught over two years, I only stayed at the college till Christmas then went back to Folkestone to study on my own, spending every day working on questions from past papers and studying model answers. Everything now depended on getting the right results!

Chapter 7

London School of Economics – from rebel to revolutionary

I was at home in Folkestone with my grandmother when the envelope arrived with my 'A' level results. I said to her, before opening it, that two B's meant the London School of Economics, a C and D meant Regent Street Polytechnic and anything less meant an end to my higher education aspirations – at least for the present. I slowly opened the envelope and pulled out the folded paper. I could hardly believe my eyes. Two Grade B's! For someone who had struggled at school only a few years earlier, this passport to one of the most prestigious universities in the world was phenomenal. My grandmother shared my elation and I hugged her and whirled her round the room!

In telling my tale I've kept saying that certain things changed my life. LSE definitely did – not only in exposing me to some superb thinkers and teachers but also in developing skills I never knew I had within the heady medium of student politics. Even before I started at LSE, I got involved in one of their demonstrations – this one against the Unilateral Declaration of Independence (UDI) in November 1965 by the white minority government of Ian Smith in Rhodesia.

During this demo, we were walking along The Strand when a black student was grabbed by a policeman. I felt he had been picked on simply because he was black. I ran up to the policeman to remonstrate. The next thing I remember was being slammed into the back of a police van, and as other people on the march started brawling and being arrested, they were being thrown in alongside me. Before I knew it, Mike McKenna was in the van as well, and without a moment's pause he said, "Quick, change coats and put my glasses on, and they'll never know who we are!"

Everyone in the van started doing just that and when we got to Bow Street police station the police officers walked up and down trying to identify us. One policeman said, "Who did I arrest?" Mike's plan had obviously worked. The policeman said, "Who got carried into the police van?" As this had happened to me I concluded that I was the one and my expression must have given me away. He said, "Oh, it was you was it?" I didn't say anything but just waited to see what he would charge me with. He said, "You were in a group lying down in front of the van and refused to move." I concluded that a charge of obstruction was better than various possible alternatives so said nothing.

The demonstration made it to the front page of the Sun newspaper the following morning. The photograph on the front page was of a policeman, his number clearly visible, arresting McKenna. He happened to be the one who had charged me.

Later that morning we were in court. I was up first and McKenna was due up after me. The policeman who had charged me, a really nice guy, started giving evidence. He talked about me laying down in front of the police van, then him making the arrest and putting me in the van. I had the copy of the Sun, and I asked him how many people he'd arrested the previous day. "Just one", he said – "you". I then asked if I could submit the newspaper as an exhibit.

The magistrate could see that the person being arrested clearly wasn't me, and I said to the policeman, "So, you arrested this chap, and he was the only person you arrested, and it obviously isn't me, so it couldn't have been me that you arrested, so I'm not guilty!"

The magistrate looked at me over his glasses and said, "So what were you doing then?" "I'd rather not say, your worship!"

"Right then, I find you guilty, and I'm fining you two pounds!" With that he banged his wooden gavel down on the block and called for the next case. I was extremely relieved. McKenna was up next and we reversed the process. Mike came in and did the same thing, He said he'd been arrested for laying down in front of a police van and therefore he couldn't have committed the offence he had been charged with - being in a group of people who refused to disperse. He was fined the same minimal amount and that was that. This episode, and the ensuing social gatherings with those involved, meant that I was already well integrated with LSE student activists by the time I joined the university in the autumn.

There were ongoing protests at LSE against the appointment of a new director, Dr Walter Adams. Students opposed him because of his alleged collusion with Ian Smith's racist regime in Rhodesia where he had been the director of University College, Salisbury. In due course the LSE campaign against Walter Adams triggered a wave of nationwide student demonstrations which, in turn, foreshadowed later international protests over such things as the war in Vietnam and apartheid in South Africa.

Meanwhile, the normal business of the university continued. LSE had a well-deserved reputation for the quality of its academic staff. Two of the most prominent at the time, from opposing political positions, were Sir Karl Popper, the conservative philosopher renowned for his opposition to communism as spelt out in his book, *The Open Society and its Enemies*, and the Marxist theorist Dr. Ralph Milliband, whose book, *Parliamentary Socialism*, argued that there was no parliamentary road – only working class revolution could achieve socialism – a view apparently not shared by his famous sons David and Ed Milliband.

We benefitted greatly by listening to as many opposing ideas as possible. Before Popper's lectures one of his minions would enter the lecture theatre to open the windows and clean the board. Then the great man would bustle in and speak with enormous energy and pace. Ralph Milliband, on the other hand, would deliver his lectures in deep and sonorous tones which those of us attuned to his message found compelling and inspiring.

The Friday afternoon meetings of the LSE Student Union were extraordinary learning experiences. Motions would be proposed and discussed by the various political and other groupings and the forum was renowned for the cut-and-thrust of debate and the merciless and constant heckling. I remember the first time I made a contribution

– not what I said but the speed with which I was overwhelmed by the opposition from the floor. As soon as I paused for emphasis the cries would go up "Can't hear you". "Speak up". "Next please".

I learnt quickly. I made sure I knew in advance the points I wanted to get across, I used the established public speaking technique of, 'tell them what you're going to tell them, tell them – and tell them what you've told them' – and I spoke loudly and fast with no pauses which would have allowed the opposition to intervene. The skills learnt in this setting proved valuable in later life, both politically and professionally.

These weekly Student Union meetings provided the main focus for the campaign against the Adams appointment. All students were automatically enrolled into the Student Union. In addition, students could join other student societies. My previous encounters with LSE students led me to join the Socialist Society (Soc.Soc) which had been established in October 1965 as a result of disillusionment with the more moderate Labour Society and which published a lively polemical magazine 'The Agitator'.

Active within Soc.Soc. were many individuals who became firm friends – two of the most energetic were Steve Jeffreys and Joan Smith, always to be found when circumstances required initiative and leadership. Laurie Flynn, a Scotsman whose father was Vincent Flynn, President of the print union SOGAT, only had to make a speech in his rich Glaswegian accent to win over the waverers. One of my closest friends and collaborators was John Rose, who in 1967 had to choose between the

Arab cause and his Jewish origins in the 6-day Middle East war. He came down on the Arab side which marked the start of his lifelong commitment to Palestinian rights on which he became a considerable authority.

In October 1966 an Agitator publication appeared entitled 'LSE's New Director – A Report on Walter Adams'. This included material from a variety of sources and was highly critical of Adams. There followed some written exchanges between the Student Union President, David Adelstein, and the Chair of Governors, Lord Bridges, on whether the criticisms of Adams were justified. Lord Bridges then wrote to the Times in support the appointment but Adelstein was refused permission to write on behalf of the Student Union to register concerns. He wrote nevertheless and as a result he faced a disciplinary hearing.

A Board of Discipline was convened and a hearing was held on 21st November. The Student Union resolved by 516 votes to 118 to deplore the action of the authorities and to hold a boycott of lectures and a peaceful demonstration. A group of students also held a sit-in outside the room where the hearing was taking place. The result was that Adelstein was found guilty but no penalty was imposed on this occasion. However, this episode was a precursor of far more serious things to come before long.

On 31st January 1967 there took place a most tragic incident. Marshall Bloom, President of the Graduate Students Association, had booked a meeting for 4pm in the Old Theatre, the spacious meeting-place where all large meetings took place. Anonymous leaflets began to appear stating that the meeting was an opportunity to discuss how to stop the Adams appointment. Reference was made to direct action.

The LSE director, Sir Sydney Caine, was informed of the leaflet and decided to ban the meeting. With most students unaware of this, by 4pm they were gathering in the main LSE entrance hall, immediately outside the Old Theatre. In the confusion which arose, Marshall Bloom and the Student Union president, Dave Adelstein, intervened to try to get a decision on whether to proceed with the meeting in defiance of the ban or to move to the Student Union bar, which was outside the Director's authority and which had already been set up with microphones in anticipation of having to be used as an alternative venue.

However, by this time a small group of students had pushed past the porters who had been ordered to stop people entering the Old Theatre. At this point another porter, Ted Poole, who had been taking a tea break nearby, came over to assist his colleagues. He was 64 years old, near retirement and described as 'having a weak heart'. He was popular with staff and students He was not physically involved in the pushing taking place but nevertheless, in the fevered atmosphere, he collapsed and died.

The impact on everyone at LSE was devastating. Sydney Caine ensured that everything necessary was done in relation to Ted Poole's family and was keen to stress that students were not to blame for the death, though this interpretation was not shared by all in the bitter recriminations which followed.

I myself was overcome by the feeling that if protest could lead to anyone's death it was not worth the price. However, in the days which followed, the view was increasingly articulated that protest, including direct action, was fundamental to progress. The civil rights struggle in America, the campaign against apartheid in South Africa and cases of repression in Eastern Europe were cited.

The upshot was that LSE set up a committee of enquiry which led, in due course, to a disciplinary hearing against Adelstein and Bloom for disobeying the Director's decision to call off the 31st January meeting. The final meeting of the Board of Discipline took place on Monday 13th March. It found Adelstein and Bloom guilty and suspended them from the university for the remainder of the academic year.

In the Old Theatre about seven hundred students waited to hear the verdicts. By then, following earlier Student Union debates, there was something of a consensus that the banning of the 21st January meeting had been unjustified and that Adelstein and Bloom had been picked on because they were the elected representatives of the students, having played relatively minor roles in the unfolding of events on the day.

When the verdicts were announced the reaction was immediate. A call for the reinstatement of Adelstein and Bloom was carried by acclamation. There was a general desire for a demonstration of protest but doubt as to its form. The new Student Union President, Peter Watherston, who was also President of the LSE Conservative Society, made a speech saying that if a protest was to be effective it must be organised and suggested a vote on whether there should be a sit-in that day, the following day or in the near future.

There is a meticulous and authoritative contemporary account of the whole period by the then Secretary (effectively Chief Administrative Officer) of LSE, Mr. Harry Kidd in his book *'The Trouble at LSE 1966-67'* in

Ted Parker in leather jacket at the LSE sit in

which I am briefly mentioned. He wrote:

While he (Watherston) was speaking Parker announced that he was now going to start a sit-in; several members left with him. Watherston then proposed two motions that were carried by an overwhelming majority: 'That the Union have a boycott until the sentences are rescinded,' and 'That this Union supports the principle of holding a sit-in.' He suggested that those who wished to organise the sit-in should go to the Union Council Room after the meeting, but Adelstein said the obvious thing to do, having decided to sit in, was to do it immediately. The meeting then broke up, but the sit-in had already started; when Parker and his companions left the meeting they had gone to the entrance hall and sat down.

The sit-in went on for many days and attracted enormous press and TV coverage, no doubt enhanced by the proximity of LSE to Fleet Street, where all the national newspapers were based at the time, and to the nearby Independent Television News studios. The campaign to reinstate Adelstein and Bloom attracted widespread support from other universities culminating in a two thousand-strong march from LSE to a mass meeting in Lincolns Inn Field which was addressed by Student Union officials and sympathetic Members of Parliament. Discussions within LSE eventually resulted in a compromise whereby the suspensions were lifted as a consequence of conciliatory comments by Adelstein and Bloom.

The normal work of the university resumed at the start of the summer term. However, militancy was in the air and protests took place at many other universities. At LSE a revolutionary group with Trotskyist origins, the International Socialists (IS) – later to become the Socialist Workers Party -

Tony Cliff

became the main beneficiary of the heightened political awareness. Its charismatic leader, Tony Cliff, became a regular visitor and encouraged the involvement of IS recruits in working class struggles beyond the campus. I joined during this period and remained actively involved for several years – years which became increasingly turbulent as protests spread more widely.

March 17th 1968 saw the so-called Battle of Grosvenor Square, a near-riot against the war in Vietnam which was covered by TV throughout the world and which contributed in due course to the war-weariness which led to the American withdrawal. LSE was again taken over by students – this time for use as a medical centre during the demonstration.

In May 1968 events in France seemed for a few extraordinary weeks to answer the wildest dreams of revolutionaries everywhere – certainly among LSE students who promptly sent emissaries across the channel in support. Students at the Sorbonne in Paris had become involved in clashes with the police during which they had torn up cobblestones to form barricades. This provoked a spontaneous response by young workers who undertook factory occupations in industry after industry to the extent that there were soon 10 million on strike, albeit with unspecified demands.

Of all things, it was the French Communist Party with its control of the trade unions which was able in due course to channel these massive protests into reformist demands for pay increases rather than the revolutionary demands for workers' control of industry being advocated by student leaders. Shortly afterwards, elections were held which returned de Gaulle to power, extinguishing any lingering hopes for radical change.

There was a bizarre postscript to the 1967 LSE sit-in. During the 1968-69 Christmas vacation the college authorities installed seven sets of iron gates at various locations within the university so that parts of it could be sealed off in the event of disruption. The Student Union called for the removal of the gates and immediately after a meeting on 24th January a task force set off with the intention of actually carrying out their removal. As it made its way round the building it encountered groups of staff standing in front of the gates to protect them. This did not stop the procession and within half an hour all the gates had been removed, never to return.

However, this was just the beginning of 25 turbulent days which dwarfed anything seen in the 1967 sit-in. 100 police entered the building and formed a cordon through which all the students on the premises were required to walk whilst staff identified anyone they could see who was involved in the event. 25 were arrested in this way. The Director then closed LSE until further notice.

Soon afterwards the students marched from LSE to the University of London building in Malet Street which they took over, declaring it 'LSE in exile'. The largest ever meeting of the Student Union eventually took place in Friends Meeting House on the Euston Road following which, despite a huge reaffirmation of opposition to the installation of the gates, the LSE authorities decided to reopen the institution, albeit in a continually troubled atmosphere.

There were several external incidents in which I became involved – even my sleepy old home town of Folkestone provided unlikely opportunities, usually during the university's summer vacations when I went back to earn good money – negotiated by the National Union of Seamen - doing 12-hour shifts on the Dover to

Calais cross-channel ferries.

On one occasion someone had booked Tariq Ali, a prominent left-wing activist, to speak at F o l k e s t o n e T e c h n i c a l College. When he arrived he was told that the college authorities had banned the

Tariq Ali addresses students at Folkestone.
Credit: John Field

meeting. The organisers promptly moved it to an adjacent barn where he addressed a couple of hundred people. The annual Folkestone Carnival happened to be assembling in nearby Shorncliffe Road. Immediately outside the college was, by chance, a float badged up as 'Student Power'. When the procession set off we joined it as it threaded its way through Folkestone. As it neared Folkestone Harbour, on its way down Tontine Street, our group broke away to go into an Indian restaurant which had set its premises aside to welcome Tariq Ali and friends for a slap-up meal which we enjoyed enormously.

Something else which led me to make an unexpected journey home was an inside story in a national newspaper headed 'Riots in Folkestone High Street'. The police had mounted some kind of

Demonstration against the arrests in Folkestone

raid and there had been a reaction from young people which spilled over into widespread fighting and mass arrests. The political types who frequented the coffee bar and pub at the centre of the disturbances began to prepare posters denouncing the police actions. I joined them, went out into the High Street carrying one of the placards and promptly got arrested. I spent the night in police cells but was quickly released after a brief court appearance the following morning.

A less dramatic but, in its way, still significant event, followed. My new-found allegiance to the International Socialists led me to invite its leader, Tony Cliff, to one of the meetings which were still being held at Mrs. Hatfield's house. However, I had not counted on Mrs. Hatfield's devotion to orthodox communism. When Cliff was in full flow with his Trotskyist denunciation of the Soviet Union Mrs. Hatfield stormed into the room to say he had to leave – so we all left! This ended a long and productive association which had enabled many of us to learn a bit more about the world around us.

Many of the events which had so absorbed my energies and interests whilst at LSE might, in retrospect, be reasonably regarded as youthful and somewhat foolish self-indulgence. However, something else happened which was altogether more serious.

In May 1967, immediately after the big LSE sit-in, I had been approached by someone called Ronnie Kasrils, a South African student who was an active member of the banned African National Congress (ANC). South Africa was undergoing extreme repression in order to maintain its brutal and racist apartheid system. Nelson Mandela, leader of the ANC, had been jailed in 1962 and was destined to languish in prison for a further 27 years.

Ronnie asked me if, in view of my support for the rights of the African people, I would be prepared to go on an undercover mission to South Africa. I considered this for a few moments then said that I would go.

Chapter 8

South Africa – an undercover mission

A lot happened during my three years (1966-69) at the London School of Economics. I've got mixed feelings about some of what we got up to but there's one episode of which I'm enormously proud. A number of us were able to play a small but significant role in the fight against apartheid in South Africa.

At the time we were sworn to such secrecy that none of us knew of the others involved. We also, somewhat surprisingly, remained absolutely silent thereafter. However, many years later, in 2012, the story was finally revealed in a fascinating book edited by Ken Keable, 'London Recruits – the secret war against apartheid', which contained the personal accounts of over 30 of those involved, including myself.

The South African apartheid system, under which the majority black population was denied the most basic of rights and kept in subjection by a white-run police state, was reviled by many in Britain who felt a degree of responsibility for South Africa as a member of the British Commonwealth. In June 1959 the Boycott Movement was established in the UK to put pressure on the South African government by boycotting the country's produce. There was widespread support from students, trade unions and the Labour, Liberal and Communist parties.

Following the Sharpeville Massacre of 21st March 1960, in which the South African police killed 69 and injured 180 following a peaceful demonstration against the Pass Laws, which restricted black people's movements, the Boycott Movement changed its name to the Anti-Apartheid Movement. This grew into a large and highly effective protest organisation. South Africa left the British Commonwealth in May 1961.

At the same time as the Anti-Apartheid Movement was building support in Britain, the African National Congress (ANC) was growing in South Africa, becoming the main political voice of black South Africans. The formal imposition of apartheid – institutionalised racial segregation – had begun following the election victory of the Afrikaner-based National Party in 1948 and gathered pace throughout the 1950's. The ANC grew in response. Following the 1960 Sharpeville Massacre the ANC abandoned non-violence and committed itself to a campaign of sabotage, in which the ANC leader Nelson Mandela took part. He was subsequently sentenced to life imprisonment.

The Sharpeville Massacre was also the event which led a 21 year old South African, Ronnie Kasrils, to join both the ANC and the South African Communist Party. His own personal story is extraordinary and includes narrowly evading arrest through all kinds of subterfuge whilst in South Africa. His activities led him to leave South Africa and he emerged in London in 1965, enrolling at the London School of Economics in autumn 1966. He did not seem unusual. LSE welcomed mature students from across the globe, many of whom had extraordinary tales to tell. In the mid-1960s these included Americans avoiding military service in Vietnam as well as exiled members of opposition movements in Rhodesia and South Africa.

In May 1967, in the immediate aftermath of the highly publicised LSE occupation, Ronnie approached me with an extraordinary proposal. "You've been very vocal in your opposition to racial oppression in southern Africa. Would you be prepared to go undercover to South Africa to help black people in their struggle?"

Faced by this moral pressure – and indeed by the intriguing prospect of going abroad for the first time in my life – I said that I would go, depending on precisely what I would be expected to do. Thus began a period during which I was briefed, trained and equipped by the ANC through Ronnie. I much later found out that I was the first person to be recruited in what became a long campaign involving firstly LSE students then, a little later, members of the London Communist Party

Ronnie rightly feared surveillance by the South African security forces even though we were in the UK so we held our initial discussions in open parkland and our later training – in things such as how to avoid leaving fingerprints, how to disguise your appearance, how to avoid pursuit and how to assemble primitive timing devices – in safe accommodation unconnected to either of us.

Ronnie also suggested that the chances of avoiding notice in South Africa would be increased by travelling with a female colleague as a couple. Ronnie and I discussed various options from among other LSE students and settled on Sarah Griffith, daughter of renowned LSE law professor John Griffith. She had been involved in the university's student protests and had been calm and resourceful throughout. It was agreed that Ronnie would explain the situation to her. She agreed to go.

The mission was to get ANC propaganda material into Johannesburg and to deploy it in various ways. We were to travel by scheduled airline and the illicit material was to be transported in the false bottoms of our suitcases. We were to post two hundred leaflets to known ANC sympathisers then, at a pre-determined time, to release ANC banners and leaflets in the city centre. Ronnie made clear that we were not to speak about the mission before, during or afterwards. "You should only do so", he said with his usual self-assurance "once South Africa is liberated". To do otherwise, he said, would endanger others involved in similar operations.

Ronnie showed us the suitcases to be used. They had check-patterned internal linings intended to confuse the eye if opened by customs officers. A false bottom in the same material was to hide thousands of leaflets, two ANC flags ('black for the people, green for the land and gold for the wealth') and three timing devices. We memorized a list of other items to purchase locally at OK Bazaar chain stores in South Africa.

We were to fly out with South African Airways, reputed to be subject to less scrutiny than other airlines by South African customs and security officers, checking in separately to increase the chances of one of us getting through if the other was arrested. When I was given my suitcase containing its hidden cargo it seemed very heavy. Even though my own belongings were fairly modest the weight greatly exceeded the baggage allowance. However, I opted to pay a surcharge rather than to transfer anything to hand luggage which would have left the suitcase looking absurdly empty if opened at customs.

The flight south was a revelation. Looking back some decades later it is amazing to reflect on just how dramatically the world has changed in terms of politics and air travel. We took off from Heathrow as dusk was falling. Our first stop was during early evening in the Portuguese capital Lisbon – then ruled by the explicitly fascist government of Antonio Salazar. In the early hours we sweltered in Angola – held in a cruel colonial grip by Portugal as part of its African empire. By early morning we had touched down in Salisbury, capital of Rhodesia, ruled by Ian Smith's white racist government in defiance of Britain and the United Nations.

It was in the transit lounge at Salisbury airport that I began to get really alarmed. Rhodesian airport magazines had headline warnings about the need for vigilance against 'red plots'. It struck me that if the South African intelligence services were as good as its opponents feared they might have got advance notice of a traveller whose recent past included internment in a military prison followed by playing a prominent role in a well publicised student revolt.

It also confirmed to me that the arrest of such a person would not be treated as an example of naïve idealism.

This, after all, was only a few years into Nelson Mandela's life sentence for 'terrorism'. My arrest, or Sarah's, would be the start of a lengthy and unpleasant ordeal. Indeed, at the outset, Ronnie had urged us, if arrested, to hold out for as long as possible so that others could remain undetected.

Our final destination was Jan Smuts airport in Johannesburg. The differences in treatment of the different racial groups became evident immediately. African porters were shouted at to carry the heavy bags, including mine. The white travelers were treated with courtesy and deference. Despite this the customs officer on my desk appeared to think seriously about asking me to open my bulging case before waving me through. It was a worrying moment.

Once on the airport bus Sarah and I linked up and made our way to a part of town recommended by Ronnie as likely to have accommodation readily available. The various manifestations of apartheid were everywhere. Separate buses for whites and non-whites. Public toilets in groups of four – white-only men, white-only women, non-white men and non-white women. Non-whites were only to be seen in menial roles. Only non-white waiters served in restaurants with white-only diners.

We soon secured two rooms in a guesthouse. This became our base for the next several days. After getting our bearings we cut the false bottoms out of the suitcases, taking care to minimize damage so that we could safely reuse the cases for our return journey. We stuffed leaflets into the pre-addressed envelopes and posted them from city centre postboxes well away from where we were staying

During the next few days we obtained the additional equipment we required including such items as wooden battens from which to suspend the flags and varnish to paint on our fingers to avoid leaving fingerprints.

Next we began our reconnaissance to locate tall city centre buildings from which the leaflets and banners could be dropped. A minor concern during this period was the heightened security arising from the presence in Johannesburg of a serial arsonist nicknamed the 'Jo'burg Firebug'. A photofit prominently featured in the local press looked uncannily like me and the description of 'ruddy complexion' fitted someone recently arrived from an English summer for a couple of weeks in a mild Johannesburg winter!

The procedure was for me to wander into various suitable buildings carrying a camera so that if challenged I could claim to be a tourist looking for somewhere to take photos. Few places seemed quite right but I eventually found two – the first was the City Treasurer's Department, one of the most prominent public buildings in town about five stories high and with a flat roof, and the second was a domestic block of flats where the dwelling at the far end of one of the balconies afforded a degree of privacy from neighbouring flats. Both met the key requirement that they were in highly visible and busy locations where the ANC flags would be seen by hundreds of passers-by before the security forces were able to respond.

We had originally hoped to identify three locations – two for the banners and another for the leaflets – but in view of our difficulty in finding suitable buildings we decided to use two only, wrapping the leaflets into the rolled-up banners so that leaflets falling into the crowded streets would cause people to look up and see the banners.

We had been instructed to get the banners to drop at precisely 3pm on a specified Friday. This necessitated packing the banners and leaflets beforehand, fitting but not setting the timing devices – these were simple clockwork alarms to which razor blades could be attached which would, in turn, cut a thread, releasing the cord fastened round the banners. We then wrapped everything up in brown paper, creating two bulky parcels about four feet long.

Having carried out the earlier reconnaissance I first approached the City Treasurer's Department on the appointed day and walked up the stairs with my large parcel to the top floor without encountering anyone. A particularly anxious moment was going up the final set of stairs to the roof, which was clearly unused with debris scattered around. A stranger going up there would be likely to cause suspicion. However, I reached the roof without incident and went over to an upturned bench, identified on my previous visit, close to the side of the building nearest to the busy main street below.

The next few minutes were the most dangerous – if anyone saw me assembling the device there would be no mistaking what I was up to. My heart was racing. First I removed the brown paper packaging, putting it into my pockets. Next I set the timer to go off at 3pm. Finally, I secured a cord to the bench and carefully positioned the package over the wall hanging down over the street where there would be no obstruction when the banner was unfurled and the leaflets went cascading down.

Whilst going down from the roof to the floor below I had a scare. Someone looking like a senior manager emerged from an office and looked directly at me whilst I was halfway down the stairs which led only to the unused roof. I was by then holding my camera and I made sure he saw it as I gave him my broadest smile and proceeded briskly to the next stairwell. He smiled back and went into a neighbouring office as I left the building.

I rejoined Sarah and we proceeded to the second building but here I encountered a snag. The secluded area of the balcony I had chosen had previously seemed suitable because the only nearby door was closed and I had concluded that the occupants were unlikely to interrupt me during the vital few minutes I needed. In the event the door opened just as I was about to unwrap the parcel and a middle-aged woman challenged me with an inquisitorial "Hello?" I responded with an incomprehensible grunt and wandered away.

On getting back to Sarah I admitted that I had no alternative location and we dumped the parcel in an alley. This was clearly a disappointment. However, Ronnie had made it clear that we should walk away if we felt threatened. The first drop was likely to have been spectacular and to have improvised something else without proper preparation would have been dangerous.

Immediately after the drop we followed our

instructions to get a late afternoon train travelling overnight to Durban and to lie low for a week before travelling back to the UK. On our return Ronnie showed us newspaper reports which indicated that the whole operation had fully achieved its objectives. Similar banners and leaflets had appeared all across South Africa, the security forces were caught completely by surprise and, above all, the ANC had demonstrated to supporters and opponents alike that it could still operate in South Africa despite the draconian measures in place to ban it.

On reflection, although our role at the time seemed both dangerous and important, what we did was insignificant compared with the later missions of the London Recruits, let alone the enormous heroism shown by those standing up against township massacres and involved in the Soweto risings - as well as the unimaginable individual courage of people such as Steve Biko, Nelson Mandela and countless others.

Despite this I am proud that LSE students had, quite literally, helped to keep the flag of freedom flying in apartheid South Africa during some of its bleakest moments. With Ronnie's permission I told my friend and fellow student John Rose what I'd done. John then carried out further missions as they became more daring and sophisticated during the following years.

Ronnie Kasrils never paused in his fight for liberation in South Africa. He continued to recruit operatives into the late 1980's and was actively involved in the struggle until apartheid was overthrown. Nelson Mandela was released in 1990. Ronnie then served in the post-apartheid government, as Deputy Minister of Defence from 1994-99, Minister of Water Affairs & Forestry from 1999-2004 and Minister of Intelligence Services from 2004-08.

I disagreed with some of his politics but admired him as one of the most tireless and committed individuals I have ever been privileged to know. His autobiography 'Armed and Dangerous' reveals how his complex and turbulent life unfolded. He was aided throughout by his courageous and principled Scottish-born wife, Eleanor, who sadly died in 2009. Ronnie has chronicled her own hugely impressive contribution in his 2010 book 'The Unlikely Secret Agent'. Both Ronnie and Eleanor were key figures in one of the most bitter and sustained battles for justice of their generation.

Chapter 9

The Battle of Lewisham – how we won

There is a mural on the wall outside Goldsmiths College in New Cross, southeast London, celebrating the highly significant 1977 Battle of Lewisham in which thousands of anti-racists blocked the route of a neo-Nazi National Front (NF) march, providing a turning point in what had seemed the relentless rise of racist politics in Britain during the 1970's.

Unfortunately the mural is an inaccurate portrayal of the event, depicting in prominent roles the Lewisham Mayor, Roger Godsiff, and the banner of the All-Lewisham Campaign Against Racism & Fascism (ALCARAF) whose organisers, though of significance in the build-up, had deliberately and publicly absented themselves from the scene some hours before the actual battle took place. I know, because I was one of the main organisers of the counter-demonstration which confronted the NF. The real unfolding of events is accurately described in the excellent book 'When we touched the sky – the Anti-Nazi League 1977-81' by Dave Renton. After Lewisham, racial politics in Britain changed completely.

But first, let's put the event in the context of the 1970's as a whole. Although the 1960's always get referred to as the decade when everything changed – student protest, flower power, the Beatles and the pill – the 1970's were probably far more significant. From student protest the emphasis shifted to widespread industrial unrest which brought down two governments – first Conservative then Labour – and arguably led to the 1979 Thatcherite revolution which dominated British politics thereafter.

In the 1950's 39.6 million working days had been lost in strike action. By the 1960's this had risen to 43.2 million. But the 1970's saw a staggering 154.8 million working days lost. This figure was never to be reached again, even in the 1980's when it was 86.4 million including 27 million in 1984 - the year of the miners' strike. By the 1990's it was down to 8.4 million, roughly where it has stayed ever since.

The strike figures reveal not only the sheer scale of industrial militancy but also the nature of working class organisation. Spearheading the revolt were the miners, whose strikes for more pay took place in 1972 and again in 1974, when the Prime Minister Edward Heath declared a three-day working week to conserve coal supplies. The government then went on to call a general election on 28th February on the theme 'Who do you want to run Britain?' The answer was not them – the Conservatives lost the election and the incoming Labour government made a deal to settle the strike.

Another trend had become apparent by then – the shift in trade union power from the official leaders to the shop floor – shown by the growth in the number of shop stewards – 300,000 by 1975 – and the increase in the number of small-scale unofficial strikes. This led to the main preoccupation of the politicians of both parties in the 1970's - to restrict the power of the trade unions – particularly the shop stewards - to call strikes.

Government attempts to introduce anti-union legislation were defeated time and time again by trade union resistance – to Labour's 'In Place of Strife' in 1969 and again to Heath's 'Industrial Relations Bill' in 1971. In 1972 the National Industrial Relations Court agreed to the jailing of five dockworkers - the so-called Pentonville Five - for picketing. This led to the threat of a TUC-led one-day general strike and the dockers were released. The realisation was dawning that trade unionists were a power in the land, capable of inflicting serious damage on elected governments.

Another important industrial dispute was in 1977 at the Grunwick film processing plant in northwest London where Asian women fought for reinstatement after being sacked for wanting to join a trade union. With wider and wider trade union support the picket lines grew to the point where 10,000 clashed with the police, with a miner who joined the picket during heavy-handed police action declaring "I was at Saltley Gate and it was a children's Sunday picnic by the side of this". Newspapers began to appear with blank pages where printworkers had refused to print pro-management articles.

However, there were warning signs. Whilst leafleting another factory in support of the Grunwick women one morning I was confronted by one of the workers who made it clear that he was a supporter of the far-right National Front (NF). Left-wing radicalism was clearly creating a response on the right. The NF, a self declared racist and fascist political party, modelled on Hitler's National Socialists (Nazis), was gaining strength in Britain in the context of the turbulent politics of the time to the point where it was winning large votes in local and national elections, getting thousands of supporters onto demonstrations and fighting for control of the streets in its key strongholds. It was a rising force, gaining support from a wide cross-section of the population but in particular from white working class youth attracted by the cult of violence and the scapegoating of ethnic minorities for the various ills of society, real or imagined.

It was greatly assisted in this by developments within mainstream Conservative thinking. The most prominent Conservative politician to use racism to garner the support of the white working class was Enoch Powell who in 1968 made a deliberately inflammatory speech warning that immigration would lead to a situation analogous to 'The river Tiber foaming with much blood' and attributing to a constituent the view that 'In 15 or 20 years' time the black man will hold the whip hand over the white man.' At a stroke he legitimized and popularised racism and his sacking from the Shadow

Cabinet by Conservative leader Edward Heath merely made him a martyr and hero.

His dismissal provoked widespread protests, including sympathy strikes and a march on Parliament by London dockworkers and meat porters. I, as part of a group of LSE students, mingled with the marchers, giving out leaflets opposing their actions and promoting a forthcoming May Day march to be led by Fleet Street printworkers and arguing for workers' solidarity. We got a mixed reception – but the May Day march was a great success!

In due course Enoch Powell moved on to become a Northern Ireland MP and his impact on British politics waned. However, his racist contribution had made its mark and fed into the increasing influence of the National Front which, by the mid-seventies, appeared to be on the point of eclipsing the Liberals as the third most popular British political party.

Soon the NF felt strong enough to go on the offensive against its far left opponents as well as against ethnic minority groups and individuals. I was a member of the Socialist Workers' Party (SWP) which had been selling its Socialist Worker newspaper for several years on Saturdays in Lewisham market. During 1977 NF members started to sell their own paper at the same time and began to attack the SWP sellers both at the street sales and at their homes. By summer 1977 the numbers on both sides had grown, with dozens of supporters travelling from other parts of London.

There was a parallel development. In May 1977 the

police in Lewisham undertook a number of dawn raids to arrest young black people suspected of 'muggings' – street robberies. The raids were highly publicised and intended to signal that the police were taking firm action against a crime which had become the subject of graphic tabloid newspaper coverage.

The nature of the raids outraged the black community. Doors had been smashed, youngsters dragged out of bed and racial abuse alleged. Parents were vocal in their opposition to the police action and a 'Lewisham 21 Defence Committee' was formed to co-ordinate legal action on behalf of the twenty-one defendants. The SWP became heavily involved in this campaign and supported the parents in organising a protest demonstration through Lewisham on 22nd July.

The demonstration was to set off from Clifton Rise in New Cross, close to the home of one of the defendants, and to make its way to central Lewisham via a circuitous route encompassing the homes of the other defendants. In the event the demonstration was a near disaster. As it gathered in Clifton Rise, a crowd of some 200 NF supporters surged out of a nearby pub where they had gathered and attacked the demonstrators with iron bars and other weapons. It was left to the police to regain some kind of order and the march straggled on its way, pursued throughout by jeering NF thugs.

After this the NF decided to follow up their victory by organising their own 'anti-mugging' demonstration, scheduling it for three weeks later – on Saturday 13th August – assembling at the same spot – Clifton Rise in New Cross. The battle lines could not have been more clearly drawn. The racist NF intended to march through an area heavily populated by black residents with slogans intended to create the maximum hostility between black and white communities. There were clear parallels with 1936 when Oswald Mosley's British Union of Fascists (BUF) had tried to march through a Jewish area of the East End but had been halted by left-wing protesters, led, at that time, by the Communist Party, in the bloody Battle of Cable Street.

In Lewisham in 1977 it fell to the SWP to organise whatever opposition it could to the NF march. At the time I was the South East London District Secretary of the SWP and I regarded it as my personal responsibility to try to provide some leadership. There were three weeks and the timing was not perfect – it was mid-summer and many reliable friends and colleagues were away. Nevertheless, we had to make a plan, get the wherewithal to deliver it and do our best to implement it effectively.

I had participated in an anti-NF mobilisation a few months earlier in Haringey, North London. This had very nearly succeeded in blocking an NF march and it provided valuable tactical lessons for what we needed to do in Lewisham. Crucially, it convinced me that the NF could, indeed, be stopped – something few others dared to believe possible. It was clear that accurate intelligence about NF plans would be extremely useful and we were fortunate as the date drew near in obtaining the exact route of the planned march together with details of police/NF contingency arrangements. This enabled us to prepare our own plans in such a way as to maximise our chances of success.

The key elements of the police/NF plan were to get the NF supporters into Clifton Rise by coach, under heavy police protection, then, heavily escorted all the way by the police, to march down to Deptford, then on to Lewisham, before marching down Lewisham High Street to Catford where they would hold a rally then disperse.

This information gave us the opportunity to devise a counter-strategy of our own, kept to as few people as possible until the last moment. This was to launch a determined onslaught on the NF march as it set off down New Cross Road but, assuming that the march got through New Cross, to get as many counter-demonstrators as possible down a more direct route to Lewisham town centre via the A20 Lewisham Way. The intention was to block Lewisham town centre, thus preventing the NF from completing their planned march.

There was, however, another group organising a protest against the NF march. This provided us with both a problem – and a great opportunity. The group was called the All Lewisham Campaign Against Racism and Fascism (ALCARAF). It was controlled by the 'Broad Left', dominated by the Communist Party but also involving local Labour Party councillors, church leaders and trade unionists. Whilst members of the SWP managed to join the organisation in the build-up to August 13th ALCARAF made clear that it was a peaceful organization and would in no circumstances allow itself to be brought into conflict with the NF march.

The main actions to which ALCARAF committed itself were to go to the High Court to try to get the NF march banned and, if unsuccessful, to organise their own march on the day itself to begin at 11.30am in Ladywell Fields in Lewisham, several miles from the NF march, and to disperse well before the 3pm start of the NF march.

The High Court refused to ban the NF march. On the day of the High Court hearing I was lucky enough to be outside the court when a BBC Radio London news team was looking for someone to comment on the decision. I was happy to oblige and gave a lengthy radio interview explaining the nature of the National Front, their aims in marching through a predominantly black area, the need to stop them and the parallels with Cable Street in 1936. I ended up by saying that I wasn't sure where Lewisham would feature on this continuum but that sooner or later we would have to stop the Nazis as our forbears did before the war, unlike in Germany where the Social Democratic Party's commitment to free speech for the Nazis resulted in all Hitler's opponents ending up in death or servitude in the concentration camps.

Once the High Court had decided that the NF march could go ahead there were a number of crucial tasks we needed to carry out. The first of these was to mobilise the local population, particularly the black youth who had been subjected to hostility by the police and the NF. In this we were greatly assisted by Tony Bogues, a prominent Caribbean political activist, who edited 'Flame', a newspaper specifically targeted at black youth. He and his team worked tirelessly in leafleting homes and meeting groups within the neighbourhood. We also worked closely with a reporter from the local Lewisham Mercury newspaper who arranged for an excellent front page clearly describing the Nazi ideology of the NF, crucial in an area which had suffered from German bombing in the living memory of many residents.

We did everything we could to build support for the ALCARAF march whilst making it clear that we would be going on to New Cross after it ended to confront the NF. Separately we purchased marine flares to be used on the day to signal when and where to break into the NF lines and we gathered up discarded fruit from Woolwich market as ammunition – this proved unnecessary as will be seen.

On the day itself it was vital to get as many people as possible from the ALCARAF march to go on to Clifton Rise in New Cross where the NF were gathering. We had lorries on the ALCARAF march with loudspeakers urging people to join us. There was opposition from ALCARAF leaders. A Labour councillor climbed into the cab of the lorry where I was speaking into the microphone and tried to stop me. I'm afraid I was rather impolite and he slipped away. A Communist Party leaflet was handed out stating 'We totally oppose the harassment and provocative march planned by the SWP'. Nevertheless, hundreds if not thousands went on to New Cross, evading police cordons.

When the police stopped the ALCARAF march the Lewisham Mayor, Roger Godsiff, made an eloquent address to the police commander about the nature of the NF, then left, together with the other ALCARAF leaders. Some presumably took the advice of the Communist Party and went to church to pray for peace!

Red Saunders, a key organiser of 'Rock Against Racism', is quoted in Dave Renton's book as saying, "What I really remember is all these Christians and Communists telling us to go home. Most people stayed. But we were all just milling about, when this old black lady, too old to march, came out on her balcony. She put out her speakers, as loud as they could, playing 'Get up, stand up'. That did it for me."

At New Cross there were already huge crowds. Angus MacKinnon, a journalist on the New Musical Express, wrote, 'On the day I arrived at New Cross and couldn't get any further. It was about eleven o'clock and there were already a lot of people there. It said in the press the next day that there were three thousand, but it must have been twice that number'.

The numbers grew ever larger as the 3pm time for the NF march to set off drew nearer. When it did the anti-racist demonstrators pushed through the police lines and halted the march. But the police pushed the crowds back and the shaken NF marchers proceeded on their way. By this time all kinds of missiles including bricks from an adjacent building site and at least one dustbin were raining down on them.

The NF march proceeded down New Cross Road and Lewisham Road towards Lewisham, coming under attack at various points. The police blocked the main mass of anti-racists from following them. At this point it became necessary to do something counter-intuitive – to lead the anti-racist demonstration away from the NF in order to backtrack left onto Lewisham Way and then to surge downhill all the way into Lewisham, breaking through police cordons on the way where necessary.

The map below helps to explain what happened next:

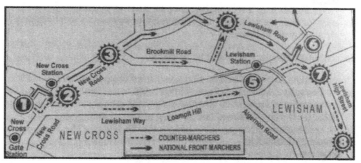

Credit: Sunday Times with numbered flash-points

In Lewisham the demonstrators merged with the huge numbers already there, creating an impenetrable wall in Lewisham High Street. This happened well before the NF, marching on their longer route, arrived. As soon as they saw the vast numbers blocking their way they stopped and were directed by the police into a tiny car park where they made a few speeches before being led through a foot-tunnel to where their coaches had been re-directed to meet them on Blackheath.

The anti-racist demonstrators remained in central Lewisham, waiting for confirmation that the NF had dispersed. However, the police lost patience and repeatedly charged, eventually and rather bizarrely using perspex riot shields for the first time on mainland Britain following their earlier use in Northern Ireland. It was at this point that I was knocked over and trampled underfoot. I had been using a loudhailer to rally the crowd into standing firm beside Lewisham clock-tower in case the NF were still around.

The next thing I knew was that I was in a hospital bed. I didn't know which hospital I was in or even what day it was. Gradually my memory returned and I pieced together that it was night-time following the August 13th demonstration, that there had been rioting in Lewisham, that afterwards I had been found wandering aimlessly about by SWP friends and that I had asked them not to take me to Lewisham Hospital in case the police arrested me and that they had instead taken me to St. Thomas' Hospital in Southwark where I was found to have concussion and broken ribs. I then phoned my wife, Britt, only to be told that I had been doing this repeatedly for several hours!

This was not the end of the National Front – but it was the beginning of the end. The Callaghan government began to ban marches where there was a risk of disorder. This defeated the NF aim of 'gaining control of the streets' and by the 1979 general election their vote was falling away. NF leader Martin Webster was quoted as saying "Our back was broken in Lewisham". In contrast, the morale of the anti-racist movement was sky-high and this was expressed in the enormous numbers – hundreds of thousands – who joined the Anti-Nazi League (ANL) and attended Rock Against Racism (RAR) concerts. The youth – black and white – had been won to the anti-racist cause and the NF gradually declined into obscurity.

One other SWP initiative worth mentioning is the Right to Work Campaign which attempted in 1975 and 1976 to create resistance to unemployment by organising marches of the unemployed, notably one from Liverpool to London culminating in a 5,000-strong rally at the Albert Hall. One of the marchers whom I had got to know beforehand was a charismatic Nigerian man, Danny Evaristo, who I visited on many occasions at his home in Plumstead, near to where I was living.

He proved to be one of the most popular speakers at the Albert Hall rally, joking that the police had claimed after an altercation during the march that he couldn't have been subjected to injury because they couldn't see any bruises. "Of course you can't see any bruises" he claimed to have told them, to great laughter and applause from the Albert Hall audience, "Because my skin is black!"

It was only much later that I realised that the young girl I had seen in the room when I came to visit Danny and his wife might well have been one of their daughters, Bernadine Evaristo, who became the wonderfully talented 2019 Booker Award-winning writer. In her fabulous book 'Girl, Woman, Other' she even makes mention of the father of one of the characters selling Socialist Worker in Lewisham market!

In terms of race, Lewisham was an important victory which paved the way for some significant changes in the wider society.

Industrial conflict continued unabated. For the Left this appeared to illustrate the 'crisis of capitalism' and herald the prospect of socialist transformation led by militant workers. However, the so-called 'Winter of Discontent' in 1978/79, when widespread strike action left rubbish piled up in the streets and bodies left unburied, undoubtedly contributed to a desire for order which brought Margaret Thatcher to power on 4th May 1979 and changed the British political landscape for the foreseeable future.

Chapter 10

Family Life

I met my first wife, Britt, in 1964 whilst I was singing at a folk club in the New Metropole Hotel, Folkestone. Britt's rather exotic full name was Brigitte Anne Lucienne Usher – her mother was a French-speaking Belgian who had met Britt's father, Derrick, whilst he was stationed with the RAF in Belgium at the end of the Second World War. They settled in Capel-le-Ferne, near Folkestone. Derrick took up teaching and Adrienne became a nurse. They had three children, Britt, Melville and Yvonne.

Britt was a talented artist and considered going to art school before enrolling at Avery Hill Teachers' Training College in Eltham, south east London, in autumn 1966 which was when I enrolled at LSE. We stayed closely in touch, spending weekends together whilst we studied for the next few years, Britt topping up her teacher training course with a Bachelor of Education (B.Ed) year at Goldsmiths College, New Cross, and me doing a one year Certificate in Education (Further Education) course at Garnett College, Roehampton, during 1970-71.

We were married on 31st July 1971 at Folkestone Registry Office, and had a small reception in a nearby pub. We were keen to live in London. Britt got a job at Deptford Park Infant School and I was appointed as a lecturer at Woolwich College. In due course we bought a semi-detached house in Merriman Road near Charlton.

After a few years Britt became pregnant with twins. We were delighted and I took to showing off the scan photos at work. Then a terrible tragedy occurred when Britt suffered a miscarriage at seven months. I was called from work in time to join her in a frantic ambulance journey to Kings College where the hope was that the babies could be saved but the consultant immediately said that it would not be possible and the twin boys died after a few minutes. We were absolutely devastated. Thankfully there were happier times ahead. We were delighted when our daughter Emma was born in 1979 followed by our son Joel in 1981.

At this time I was still heavily involved with the Socialist Workers' Party and my anti-racist activities began to attract increasingly hostile attention from the far-right National Front. We decided to move and we were lucky enough – so we thought – to find a run-down but rather grand four-storey house in the middle of fashionable Blackheath which we set about renovating. It was then that we discovered that it was full of dry rot, undetected by the building society survey, and the resulting expensive remedial work plunged us deep into debt which we could ill afford.

The children were everything. Every day there was something to sort out or enjoy. They both went to nearby John Ball primary school. I have a memory of Emma, aged five, sitting in our kitchen cutting up a loaf to make sandwiches for her lunch so she could use her dinner money to buy sweets!

Sadly, Britt and I began to drift apart and by the mid 1980's we took the heart wrenching decision to separate. The children were only young – four and six – and I have no doubt that for Britt, as much as for me, the sense of guilt was deep and enduring. It was a horrible time. One positive factor, probably the only one, was that house prices had surged and our rather tawdry house had become the highly desirable residence we had initially envisaged. The result was that when we sold it there was sufficient money for Britt to buy a house with enough room for the children and for me to buy somewhere as well.

At that time I had a friend who'd been in a similar situation and after he split up with his wife he made sure he found somewhere to live very close to his children so that he could maintain good relationships with them. On his advice I did the same and got a small terraced house in Lewisham within walking distance of Britt's and with bedrooms for each of the children. Britt and I agreed an arrangement whereby we each had Emma and Joel for exactly half of the time.

My house at 10, Boyne Road became somewhere the children were happy to be. The children and I shared a make-believe world with Egbert the Ghost, who often floated through locked doors and walls to join us in mysterious adventures. There was even a theme tune: 'Egbert the Ghost, Egbert the Ghost – all the children love Egbert the Ghost'.

There were relaxed occasions when we watched popular TV sit-coms together and succumbed to fast food and Indian takeaways. However, it is a tribute to their innate good judgement, and no doubt that of their mother, that they emerged into adulthood with admirable character traits combining, in different ways, honesty, commitment and a positive approach to healthy eating and the environment.

At one stage I took to popping down to Folkestone for weekends to stay at my mother's house with the children and enjoy the seaside. I have a particular fond memory of driving back from the beach one day and seeing a board advertising an evening football match between Folkestone Invicta and Brighton & Hove Albion. The five or six year-old Joel had started to show an interest in football on TV and I decided to take him to the game.

It was a magical evening. There were not many spectators and we were able to stand at the fence surrounding the pitch. There was a beautiful pink moon and the wonderful smell of hot dogs. Then, astonishingly, as the game started, young Joel, who didn't usually communicate very much at that stage, began in a loud and clear voice to deliver a rapid-fire commentary on the game, using the match programme combined with the players' shirt numbers – something along the lines of "It's Smith to Jones, the pass intercepted by Adams…." I started to hush him up out of embarrassment then realised what an extraordinary feat I was witnessing!

Many years later I saw a development of this at Charlton Athletic where he could converse with anyone in the crowd about any aspect of the team including which player had scored which goal in which game against which opponent. He was a sporting encyclopedia, which proved invaluable in providing him with a passion and interest.

As will become clear, Joel and I owe much to my second wife, Jennifer for introducing us to Charlton Athletic. Jennifer and I met in Somerset in 1993 on a residential course. It was a Masters in Business Administration (MBA) course specifically designed for Further Education managers. I was a college principal in London at the time and Jennifer was a head of department at Accrington & Rossendale College in Lancashire. I was immediately attracted to her. On the first evening the whole group – British and, to my surprise, Danish college managers – walked down the hill from the campus – the Mendip Centre – to a pub a mile or so away.

As we entered the pub I noticed a piano and began to play and sing some rock 'n roll songs. Most of the group edged away but Jennifer joined in, confirming my instinct that this was someone I might get on with. The course was delivered in one-week residential modules over two years and we both got together soon after it started. It transpired that both our marriages had ended several years earlier and we began a long-distance courtship, meeting up every couple of weeks either in London or at Jennifer's home in Oldham.

When Jennifer first came to visit me in London there was an incident which might well have been a warning to her. When it was time for her to go back to Manchester we travelled by train and tube to Euston station so that she could catch one of the hourly inter-city trains north. As we got near to Euston I realised that if we were quick we could catch a train an hour before the one we had in mind. However, as we got to the underground ticket barrier my ticket failed to operate the exit gate.

Furious, and with many expletives, I dived through the small aperture where suitcases could be pushed through, then ran to the departure platform, just failing to get onto the platform before the attendant pushed the gate shut. I then ran from platform to platform trying to get through as the attendant ran ahead of me closing each gate in turn, ignoring my shouts, whilst I shouted that he was making me lose an hour of my precious time.

Jennifer had meanwhile gone to the cafeteria and when I joined her she was convulsed with laughter saying, "I've just seen the Principal of Barking College diving through a luggage space". I saw the joke and calmed down. However, this wasn't the last time my impatience let me down at Euston station. On a subsequent occasion when her boys joined her for a visit we all went to Euston by car for the return journey. As we drew near I again realised we could get an earlier train and, on arrival at the station, I rushed the family onto the platform, the boys protesting bitterly that they had wanted to stop for magazines and refreshments! Despite this the relationship survived and thrived.

Jennifer's boys, Benjamin and Jonathan, were aged fourteen and ten at the time and despite the intrusion of a strange southerner into their mum's life they put up with me with great tolerance and good humour. Over the following years we got to know each other really well. Both Benjamin and Jonathan were, and remain, passionate supporters of Oldham Athletic Football Club, a commitment nurtured by their dad, Ron, who continued to take them to matches every weekend after he and Jennifer split up. However, the boys took the chance to go to a game without their dad when they were brought down on a visit to London with their mum in December 1994. There happened to be a game against Charlton Athletic on 17th December and Ben and Jonny were determined to go.

Joel and I had never been to a professional football match so we set off with Ben and Jonny with a degree of trepidation about what might be in store, particularly with a noisy crowd of opposition fans. As we got near the ground we were approached by a boisterous Oldham fan who asked us if we had tickets. When we told him we hadn't, he produced a handful and said, "Here, take these". Ben was immediately suspicious and whispered, "Don't take them". I asked, "How much" and the man said, "Nothing – they're players' tickets so I haven't had to pay for them". I didn't really understand what he meant but, despite Ben's misgivings, I gratefully took the tickets – and, lo and behold, we all walked through the turnstiles and into the ground!

We enjoyed the game enormously and, although Ben and Jonny ended up disappointed by Charlton's 2-0 victory. Joel and I were so taken by the excitement of the occasion that we both decided that we would like to go to future Charlton games. We became season ticket holders – and subsequently 'away' season ticket holders which meant that we also went to all the away games. We even travelled abroad to follow the team on its pre-season tours. Over time Jonathan became a strong Charlton supporter, suffering conflicting loyalties whenever the two teams played each other!

The high point for us all was when Charlton won promotion to the Premiership in a thrilling play-off match against Sunderland at Wembley on 25th May 1998 (Emma's birthday). The score after extra time was tied at 4 - 4 with Charlton going on to win 7 - 6 on a penalty shoot out. The game is sometimes described as 'the greatest play-off final ever'.

Mention needs to be made of the strong bonds within Jennifer's family, her particularly close relationship with her younger sister Gillian and the affection and esteem in which the sisters, together with their children, held their father, Frank. In a life which included wartime service in RAF Bomber Command and a later career as an inspector in the police force in Oldham he provided an excellent role model of steadfast family support and strong moral principles. He died in 2015 at the age of 91. Jennifer's mother had died in 1985 at the relatively young age of 59.

In view of the close family ties attaching Jennifer to Oldham it was therefore a momentous decision when, in 1995, she decided to move south with her two boys. She successfully applied for a vice-principalship at Newham Community College (NewVic) in London and rented a place in New Eltham. She then bought a lovely house in Strongbow Road in Eltham which I bought into when we got married in 2000. By then Jennifer had transformed the place by knocking down walls, taking out fireplaces and installing others and sorting out the kitchen and bathroom. We have both loved being there. We eventually added a conservatory, the focus of many parties and family gatherings.

The garage proved a useful repository for the many belongings which we and our children had collected. On one occasion I was on a ladder hanging a bicycle on the garage wall. The next thing I knew was that I was in an ambulance answering questions intended to see if my memory was returning. Apparently I had fallen off the ladder into a pot of paint which covered all my clothes. I then appeared at the bottom of our stairs in my underpants calling for Jennifer, having left my clothes in the garden. Jennifer called our neighbour, Sue Ring, for help and after a spell in the bath I was transferred to the ambulance. I was made to promise that I would never again go up a ladder unsupervised.

However, a few weeks later, prior to a social event, I concluded that I needed to get rid of some rubbish for which there was no room in our wheelie bin. I realised that I could create some space by jumping up and down on the contents of the wheelie bin. However, I would need to get into it using a small stepladder - and I had been banned!

I therefore got up early one morning, whilst Jennifer was still asleep, and crept out to the wheelie bin, quietly collecting the stepladder from the garage on the way. As envisaged, I climbed into the wheelie bin and began to jump up and down. However, I had failed to take into account that the bin was located on a sloping path which ran from the side of the house down to the road.

The bin began to roll down towards the road, gathering up the two other bins on the way. I had several seconds to realise that when it reached the road it would tip up, spilling out the contents including myself. I decided that the best thing to do was to stay calm and shortly afterwards I found myself on the ground. I looked around, firstly so see if anyone had observed this misfortune, then, more importantly, to see whether our bedroom curtains had moved, indicating that Jennifer had heard the commotion. Luckily no-one had witnessed the event.

I cleared up the rubbish, went back in the house and back to bed. However I was unfortunately not yet in the clear. Before long the front of my body was covered in vivid bruises. I managed to keep this from Jennifer for a few days but eventually decided that I needed to see a doctor in case I had any internal injuries. I remember waking up and saying, "Jennifer, I've been very silly and I need to see a doctor". "What have you done?" she asked, fearing the worst. When I told her the story she smiled and added it to the long list of my foolish misdemeanours. The doctor, needless to say, dismissed my fears of internal injury, saying that I would be dead by now if I'd suffered any.

Whilst the house provided a focus for our lives together, both of us actively pursued our careers – me at Barking College (see chapter 12) and Jennifer, following her time at NewVic, as Principal of John Ruskin College in Croydon. Jennifer also found, in her move to London, a great opportunity to indulge her love of theatre with the West End's theatreland only 30 minutes away by train.

As time went by the four children in our joint family got on increasingly well together and pursued their different paths with great success.

My daughter Emma had gone to John Ball primary

school in Blackheath, then Crown Woods comprehensive in Eltham before studying Economics at York University. She then made a remarkable relocation to the other side of the world to teach English in Japan. I made a visit lasting little more than a weekend and was enormously impressed by how well she had coped with living so far from home and dealing with a completely different culture and language.

On her return to the UK she got a job at the Financial Ombudsman Service near Canary Wharf where she rapidly rose to become the leader of their Communications Team. She was often to be seen on breakfast TV explaining some development or other in the world of finance.

She got married in 2008 to Ian Smillie, from an Ayrshire farming family but by then a successful figure in the demanding world of international banking. The wedding took place in Ayr with a wonderful reception a few miles away in the fabulous setting of Calzean Castle. Emma's many friends made their way to Scotland by plane for the event and were so numerous that they took up most of the seats on one flight. In fact, there were so many people at the reception that there had to be a repeat ceremony a few weeks later to accommodate the Smillie family's extensive network of friends in the Ayrshire farming community.

Joel, born in February 1981, also went to John Ball and afterwards to Crown Woods before transferring to Christ the King Sixth Form College for his 'A' levels. He applied to study Psychology at Leeds University and awaited his 'A' level results with anxious excitement. He phoned me when he got the results, delighted to inform me that he had got three A grades. He said, "This is the second best day of my life. You know what the best day was". He meant, of course, Charlton's promotion to the Premiership in 1998!

At Leeds Joel graduated with a first class degree and I was hugely impressed when he then secured a post in New York, working with adults with learning difficulties. He ended up staying there for nearly two years. I visited him twice, both times on his birthday in the freezing month of February, the first time with Jennifer and the second on my own. It was on this second visit that Jennifer's son, Ben, happened to be in New York at the same time and the three of us met up for Joel's birthday celebration in a Greenwich Village pub which was packed with Joel's friends.

When he returned to the UK he undertook further studies, gaining a Doctorate in Clinical Psychology in Guildford before starting a highly successful career as a Clinical Psychologist.

He was married in 2010 to Gulistan Kurban, a delightful and accomplished primary school teacher, originally from Turkey. They bought a house in Archery Road Eltham, conveniently close to where Jennifer and I live. Before they could move in, they needed to get the place decorated which ended up as a massive task carried out with great pace and energy as a joint project involving me, my friend Chris Witt and Gulistan's family, who travelled over from Ilford on a daily basis. We did it – just in time for the happy couple to move into their fine family home together with their first son, Reuben.

Jennifer's boys developed successful careers in their very different ways. Ben, born in 1979, was 16 when the family moved to London. He studied 'A' levels at Christ the King Sixth Form College then went on to University College, London, where he studied History. In the years that followed, Ben developed a career as an IT entrepreneur that enabled him to combine work and travel. For five years he worked for UNESCO's Oceans and Small Islands division providing IT support for their research project.

He was based in Paris but his work took him to many different countries including several in the third world. Subsequently he undertook freelance work for UNESCO and chose to live in various parts of the world from Barcelona to Cape Town. Later he settled down in East London and set up his own company - Tech City Labs - specialising in providing a wide range of data services to businesses. He also developed an active interest in politics standing twice for election for the constituency of Leyton and Walthamstow in 2016 and 2019 for the Liberal Democrat Party.

In 2020 Ben married Holly Pattenden, an Oxford educated senior manager in the energy industry. They had met whilst both were students and were a couple at that time. After they graduated they each went their separate ways but maintained a friendship throughout, finally settling down together 20 years later. Jennifer had always liked Holly and was delighted to have her as a daughter-in-law.

Jonathan, Jennifer's younger son, born in 1983, went to Crown Woods comprehensive on arrival in London.

'A' level studies at sixth form college were followed by a gap year in Australia. He had a work placement in Albury-Wodonga as a teaching assistant at Wodonga High School. It says much for Jonathan's remarkable social skills that, as well as getting on with his two host families, he established excellent rapport with staff and pupils at the school. When he left he wrote a song, much performed since, called 'Bye Bye Wodonga High', sung to the tune of 'American Pie' and mentioning all the staff members by name.

Jonathan went to Hull University on his return to the UK studying History and American Studies. After this he went into the banking sector in London. Then two crucial things happened. Firstly he met his future wife, a charming and highly regarded human resources specialist, Hannah Davy and they were married in 2013. Secondly he decided that he wanted to change career to something more fulfilling – namely teaching - even if it meant earning less in the short term. He did a year's teacher training course before getting a job in a primary school in Charlton. He then moved to a neighbouring school as deputy head before becoming its headteacher.

Our four children have done much to make us proud, as have our many grandchildren – but as they were all born after my retirement I'll save their exploits till a later chapter.

Chapter 11

Working Life

Previous chapters have dealt with my working life in the RAF, TV engineering and various casual jobs. Of these, the most significant in terms of character development was the RAF with its emphasis on discipline, punctuality and smartness. However, my working life mainly comprised my 47-year career in Further Education.

I'm not sure I'd heard of Further Education colleges until someone mentioned them as a possible employment opportunity as I was leaving LSE in the summer of 1969. Even then I left it too late that year to get a teaching qualification so I applied to start a one year Certificate in Education (Further Education) course at Garnett College, Roehampton, beginning in September 1970.

That left me with a year to find something else to occupy me. I was lucky that my friend, John Rose, knew of a vacancy at a company called Media Expenditure Analysis Ltd (MEAL) which operated from Dean Street in the intriguing Soho area of London. I applied to be a delivery driver but on arrival was asked by the newly appointed Company Secretary, Eric Pimm, whether I could count.

When I said I could, I was whisked into the accounts office and before long found myself entrusted with a variety of tasks including sending out sales invoices, something which hadn't been done for several months, plunging the company into an unnecessary cash-flow crisis. I enjoyed a somewhat chaotic year during which I found out how the business worked, basically coding press and TV advertising expenditure to find out how much the top companies were spending on advertising, then selling the data in an expensive 'MEAL Digest' to commercial companies and media groups.

Because MEAL was owned by a consortium of newspapers it was regarded as an outpost of Fleet Street and soon became a target for unionisation by the print union, SOGAT. I became the shop steward or - in the quaint parlance of the print unions – Father of the Chapel (FoC) - which gave me some interesting insights into the workings of trade unions.

I began my year's teacher training at Garnett College in September 1970 and was sent to do my term of teaching practice at Woolwich College. I must have made a favourable impression because I then got a job at Woolwich as an Assistant Lecturer. I stayed there for thirteen years rising in due course to the lofty position of Senior Lecturer, Deputy Head of Department.

Woolwich College

I loved my time at Woolwich and learnt an enormous amount. However, at first I struggled. I had opted to teach 'A' level Sociology – that was fine – but also something called English & General Studies to engineering apprentices. My thinking – in line with my worthy socialist ideals – was that I would find myself discussing with the working class youth of southeast London the various ways in which society might be improved. I was quickly disabused of these fine aspirations!

The college had a strong emphasis on engineering, admirably organised by the Engineering Department – the largest of the college's four departments. It had three vocational specialisms, mechanical, motor vehicle and electrical engineering. The students were undertaking apprenticeships lasting up to five years. They were generally very enthusiastic about the vocational elements of their college courses but extremely cynical about having to spend time on something as vague as 'General Studies', which was taught in one and a half hour sessions by my own 'Department of Arts & Liberal Studies'.

The Liberal Studies Department had high credibility with other departments resulting from the professionalism of its leadership and lecturing staff. The Head of Department who appointed me was Monty Johnstone, a Communist Party member and respected writer and intellectual who had a refreshingly critical attitude to the Soviet Union. I was disappointed when he left at the end of my first year to concentrate on his writing but he was replaced by his excellent deputy, Harry Bridges, who was a committed Catholic and one of the kindest and most supportive managers I ever encountered.

My commitment to teaching apprentices proved tough for the reasons mentioned above. In my first year, as well as other teaching commitments, I was required to teach six classes of apprentices from all three vocational specialisms and from first years to fifth years. The motor vehicle students were reputed to be amongst the most resistant to General Studies and I had been timetabled to take a class designated MVM3 – Motor Vehicle Mechanics third year – from 6pm to 7.30pm on Friday evenings – the last class of their day – and of my working week. A wonderfully entertaining book, "Wilt' by Tom Sharpe, perfectly captures the ghastly if comic challenges of teaching General Studies at this time in educational history, For my 'MVM3' of motor vehicle students you can substitute Tom Sharpe's 'MEAT3' of catering students!

At Woolwich all classes were compulsory for the engineering apprentices – if they missed any without good reason they lost a day's pay. This didn't endear them to General Studies. There were about twenty in the motor vehicle class. The first time I met them I had carefully prepared what I would teach. I arranged to take two sets of books from the Liberal Studies bookstore, one a work of fiction to provide a basis for discussion and subsequent written homework, and one a set of grammatical exercises to improve their written communication skills.

Before the class started I took in one set of books and left them on the teacher's desk. The students were already in the room, milling around and looking out of the window, whistling at the girls passing by. I then went out to get the second set of books. This was my first mistake – the first of many! When I got back to the classroom the first set of books had disappeared. "Where are the books I brought in?" I asked of what now took on the aspect of a sullen gang. No-one answered until one of a pair of the only black students in the group took pity on me and said "I think they've gone out the window sir".

The room was on the first floor. I looked out of the window and saw my books – suspended from the cords attached to the room's window-blinds. At least this was better, I suppose, than them having been thrown onto the ground. However, the unedifying struggle to retrieve the books was symptomatic of my subsequent efforts to gain control of the class. Every encounter threatened to be a battle. And every one of my General Studies groups had similar dynamics.

Something had to be done – but what? At first I found myself forced to impose strict discipline, relying heavily on the authority of the Head of Engineering to back me up if any of the students refused to do what was required. However, this was not the kind of job I had anticipated – and, somewhat miraculously, I hit upon a strategy that not only enabled me to survive my first difficult year of teaching but actually earned acclaim from the rest of the department.

The college turned out to be excellently equipped with something called AVA – Audio-Visual Aids. The AVA Department had brilliant staff and every piece of technical equipment a teacher could ask for. This included sound recording equipment and film cameras using 4-minute reels of 8 millimetre film. Somehow I hit upon the idea of building my lessons round film-making projects, getting each of my six General Studies classes to research some aspect of our local area with a view to producing a four-minute film in which class members would feature, the whole thing to be enlivened by a suitable piece of recorded music.

This worked amazingly well and resulted in a twenty-four minute film entitled 'Six sketches of South East London' including such unlikely sequences as my two black students from MVM3 starring in a car chase through the newly-built Thamesmead housing estate to the theme from 'Shaft', a motorbike trip across the Woolwich Ferry to 'Proud Mary' by Creedence Clearwater Revival and a narration about the Greenwich Observatory punctuated by 'Also sprach Zarathustra', the music used in the film '2001'.

Not only did the students enter into the spirit of the project with enthusiasm but at the end of year departmental review the film received plaudits from the assembled staff members who were all experienced and successful teachers. So ended a year which began disastrously but finished with my reputation considerably enhanced.

A lot later I used a somewhat similar approach for a project of my own. After ten years' service the Inner London Education Authority (ILEA) awarded teachers a one-term sabbatical for further study. Instead I got permission to use the time to make a film about the working lives of some of our students. Among the companies covered was the Otis Elevator Company. I filmed our students carrying out maintenance work on a variety of elevators including the futuristic 'Otis Elevonic 2000', at that time the fastest lift in Europe. I got an amazing shot by persuading our Media Resources Officer, Pete Nalder, to get on the top of the lift as it hurtled up the lift shaft. Although we took great care to make sure this was done safely, in later years 'Health & Safety' would quite rightly have banned it!

After thirteen years at Woolwich College, during which time I became Deputy Head of Department, and served as Branch Secretary of the lecturers' union, NATFHE (National Association of Teachers in Further & Higher Education) and helped to embed the General Studies curriculum within the new BTEC qualifications in an approach more closely related to the vocational requirements of the students, I decided that, much as I loved being at the college, I risked being stranded there forever unless I could get a job elsewhere.

This led me to apply for a post at Head of Department level at Brixton College, also in London and within easy travelling distance of where I was living in Blackheath.

One other thing needs to be mentioned before I leave the story of Woolwich College. I found out many years later that two other people I met there turned out to have been 'London Recruits', secretly involved in the undercover mission to South Africa. One was George Bridges, a college lecturer, who at the time of the South Africa venture was District Secretary of the London Communist Party and had recruited many of those who subsequently travelled abroad. The other was Tom Bell, also a Communist Party member who was then a young Electrical Installation apprentice whom I taught in one of my General Studies classes.

Brixton College

Back to my shortlisting for the job at Brixton College.

The interview was an extraordinary experience, though as nothing compared with what was to follow. The year was 1984.

The interview process took place over two days with the first day being devoted to providing candidates with an overview of the college and the job followed by interrogations of the candidates by groups of staff and students. This was no ordinary college. It had a reputation for having been badly run, with the teachers' union, NATFHE, ruling the roost and racial antagonism between the largely white college management and the overwhelmingly black student cohort. A new woman Principal, Ulla Barlow, had taken over. Ulla was Finnish. She was busily establishing her authority by promoting NATFHE members into management positions and winning over key black staff members by actively espousing progressive anti-racist policies.

Of the candidates for the job, named 'Head of Course Group; Continuing Training & Education' most were already members of the college staff and well known to the interviewing panel. It became clear that a key task for the successful candidate would be to open a newly refurbished building a few miles from the existing college campus. This building had been made available following the highly publicised Brixton Riots of 1981 and was located in Barrington Road, near Coldharbour Lane in the heart of the riot area known as the 'Front Line'. It was intended that the site would provide vocational courses for local residents.

I had decided by the end of the first day that the job was likely to go to an internal candidate and that a white male applicant who had been at his previous college for thirteen years was not an appealing prospect. Nevertheless I decided to make the best of it and to go before the interview panel with all guns blazing. My chance came when the Vice Principal, an amiable Welshman named John Gaffikin asked what I knew to be the vital question. "Did you ever detect elements of racism at your present college and, if so, what did you do about it?".

In fact there had been many instances of racism during my time at Woolwich College and I had been instrumental in tackling the issue. I gave one graphic example. There had been a particularly unpleasant group of 'British Movement' supporters among the students on a full-time Engineering Industry Training Board (EITB) course. They stuck vile racist stickers on notice boards and even attacked black students. The Principal failed to react to this despite my entreaties so I organized a small meeting one evening during a college holiday with the Chair of Governors, John Cartwright, who was also the Labour MP for Woolwich East. I took with me one representative from each of the four college departments.

John Cartwright brought with him an aide who took notes. At first Mr. Cartwright was slightly hostile, probably uneasy about having been put in this situation. As we were explaining our feelings he suddenly interjected to say, "Look, I am sympathetic but unfortunately there are racist views everywhere, not just among your students. Why, just today there was a horrible incident near Woolwich Market where thugs were dragging Asian drivers out of their cars and beating them up – and that couldn't possibly have been your students because the college is on holiday".

I was about to nod in agreement when our Engineering Department representative, Charlie Bradley, said, "Hang on – what time was this?" "About 5pm" said the MP. "Well", said Charlie, I wouldn't want to jump to conclusions but the EITB students do a 48-week year so they were in college today and finished at 5pm so it could well have been them".

With that, the MP's attitude changed. "What would you want the Principal to have done?" he asked. "Call a meeting of the students and tell them that any racist actions will lead to their expulsion" I said. I don't know what John Cartwright did next but there was a transformation of practices within the college. Not only did the Principal convene a meeting along the lines I had suggested but officers from the Engineering Industry Training Board also attended and were equally clear that racist activities would not be tolerated.

The members of the Brixton College interviewing panel were clearly impressed by this example. I suspect that the next question settled matters. This concerned any experience I'd had in setting up a new college site. As it happened, that's exactly what I'd done in my final year at Woolwich. As a result of many years' lobbying, in which I'd been involved as NATFHE Branch Secretary, Woolwich College had been allocated extra space in the shape of a disused school site in Charlton and I opted to move there to plan and equip my department's share of the building – this included installing Art & Design studios and a Multi-skills workshop as well as playing a part in the overall management of the facility. This was exactly the kind of experience needed at Brixton – which none of the other candidates could provide.

So – I got the job. But this was just the start of three tempestuous years which began with the Principal, Ulla Barlow, pinning me against a wall and saying, "You're the wrong gender and the wrong ethnicity but you've got the job – so you'd better start making allies".

One thing which became clear immediately was that I didn't even have an office. I was told that my embryonic department – or 'Course Group' - comprising courses transferred from other departments - would be based at an Adult Education site called Elm Park. My Vice Principal, John Gaffikin, who turned out to be a real help in the chaotic world in which I found myself, said, "Let's go to Elm Park and get you an office. You'll have to deal with their Vice Principal, who's a difficult character".

When we got there John said, "This is Ted Parker, our new Head of Continuing Training & Education. He'll need an office". The response was immediate. "We haven't got an office for him. We need all our rooms for community response". I summed up the situation in a trice. I was going to have to use my wits to survive. I said, "Is there somewhere I can use on a temporary basis?" He replied, "Well, there's a common room – you can go in there to work". I readily agreed, a plan already forming in my mind.

We were close to the summer holidays. During this time the Adult Education staff, including the troublesome Vice Principal, would disappear from the site and not return till a couple of weeks after Brixton

College resumed teaching in September. I decided that the common room would become the organisational hub of my new Course Group. I had meanwhile been promised whatever funding I needed to get started. With that assurance I ordered desks and filing cabinets for my course team leaders together with a switchboard system and telephones for my soon to be appointed Administrative Officer, a cheerful young woman called Sally.

The result of all this was that when the Brixton College staff returned they had their own desks and admin support, all located within the common room. When the Adult Education staff returned a couple of weeks later they walked into their old common room to find it a hub of activity with phones ringing and staff busily sorting out their teaching resources. They looked round in confusion before withdrawing to make whatever arrangements they could for spending their non-teaching time.

I gained enormous pleasure a few days later when John Gaffikin phoned from the Brixton College main site to ask if there were any spare rooms we could use at Elm Park. I passed on the request to the Elm Park Vice Principal who went apoplectic and jumped up and down shouting, "Spare room, spare room – no, we haven't got any spare room. You move in here while we're away in this well-oiled operation and take over the place. Then you ask me if we've got any spare room! You're never, ever, going to get any more room!"

I was delighted to have my incursion described as a "well-oiled operation" but slightly alarmed about the rapidly deteriorating relationship between the two institutions. However, I unwittingly stumbled upon a bold solution to the problem. I had heard Adult Education staff say that they wished we would get out of Elm Park and go to another Adult Education enclave in Ferndale Road, which also housed the Brixton College Engineering Department.

When I mentioned this at a Brixton College management meeting Ulla Barlow became very excited, saying to John Gaffikin, "John, that's perfect. Arrange a meeting with the Elm Park Principal to tell him we'll get out of Elm Park if they'll get out of Ferndale Road". John Gaffikin arranged the meeting which I also attended and the swap was agreed. As we walked down the corridor afterwards John Gaffikin whispered to me "Not bad for a bunch of squatters!" I nearly doubled up with mirth. John was right. It was doubtful if we had any right to be in Elm Park and now we had the whole of Ferndale Road!

The next step was even more difficult than my intrusion into Elm Park. We had to move all my courses in with the Engineering Department – and the culture clash could not have been more evident. The virtually all-white engineers suddenly had to cope with a largely black group of staff and students who they perceived to be noisy and ill-disciplined. At first they tried to claim there was insufficient room for our staff (shades of Elm Park) and that the refectory could not cope with the influx of our students.

However, when I began to prepare proposals to create more space by knocking down the walls between their generously proportioned offices the objections magically disappeared. Thus, for my nomadic team, after our first year (1984-5), bonding in the hostile atmosphere of Elm Park, we marched together into our second year (1985-6) at Ferndale Road as unwelcome guests of the Engineering Department before decamping for our third year (1986-7) into our permanent home at the newly refurbished ex-school building at Barrington Road.

I have to say, being at Barrington Road was a joy. We had a wonderful mix of staff and students – Electrical Youth Training Scheme youngsters led by a superb course tutor, adults on 'second chance' Access courses covering a variety of vocational specialisms and 'Return to Learning' courses for students needing help in basic skills before progressing to the vocational options. In the year before we moved in I spent most of my time working with the staff to get the machines and other technical equipment they needed. I was particularly glad to receive an unexpected visit from the ILEA's top computer advisers who made sure we received the most up-to-date equipment for the new IT workshops.

An early decision which set the tone for Barrington Road was when the Brixton College management team asked me what security staff I would need. I said, "None". This was met with incredulity. At the main Brixton College site the security was tighter than in a military facility. To get in, students needed to press a button allowing them to enter a kind of time-vault where their ID could be checked by security guards protected by a glass screen before they would be allowed out into the college foyer.

I decided that at Barrington Road a more relaxed regime would enable the students to feel the place was theirs and that they would police it themselves. It worked beautifully and before long staff throughout the college were doing what they could to do some of their teaching at Barrington Road. I personally made sure I was visible at all times in the corridors and workshops – something I took with me when I later became a college principal. One thing that had changed by then, however, was my attitude to security. Colleges later faced huge problems with gangs and drugs and needed strict security to keep their students safe. Before I became a college principal, however, I had one more move to make.

Ulla Barlow unexpectedly left Brixton to take on the Principalship of Acton College in the West London Borough of Ealing. John Gaffikin became the Principal of Brixton College and the post of Vice Principal was advertised. I applied, but despite having got the college through some difficult times and successfully opened its new prestige site I was not shortlisted, though a number of other more junior internal candidates were. Rightly or wrongly I felt quite offended by this. However, I needn't have worried!

Within a few weeks I received an unsolicited approach from Ulla Barlow, by now well established in her new post at Acton College. She invited me to apply for the position of Vice Principal, Marketing & Special Projects. Despite not being quite sure what was entailed I duly put in an application – and got the job.

Acton College

As at Brixton, Ulla had introduced some dramatic changes and I found myself in the forefront of trying to implement them. She had sensibly left the management structure largely unchanged, unlike at Brixton where her new 'matrix system' had created considerable confusion about who was responsible for running courses – the 'Heads of Course Group' (like me) who basically created new courses and provided accommodation – and the 'Subject Team Leaders' who provided the teaching staff. At Acton the Heads of Department did both, providing clarity about who was in charge of delivering courses and ensuring high quality.

My role at Acton combined marketing the college – not as easy as it sounds when course team leaders somehow expected the marketing team to recruit students for unpopular courses which were well past their 'sell-by' date – with 'special projects', which turned out to be inventing bright ideas for making money or responding to approaches from various external agencies. The most dramatic of these approaches occurred within a few days of my appointment – from the Hotel & Catering Training Board (HCTB). They had themselves been approached by an organization called Ciao (pronounced Chow) Italia, representing all the main Italian restaurant chains in the UK. Ciao Italia's Chief Executive rejoiced in the unlikely name of Mr. Taverna. We got to know him extremely well.

His idea was to find a college which could become the UK's centre for Italian restaurant training in the UK – and he had settled on Acton College. Ulla was delighted, despite the fact that Acton College had no experience of catering training and no suitable training facilities. In fact, encouraged by the HCTB, she envisaged not only that Acton could become the focal point for the training of Italian restauranters but that, when not in use by the Italians, these yet to be developed facilities could be made available for training in other national cuisines such as French or Scandinavian.

At this point it is necessary to pause for a moment to reflect on how space happened to be available at Acton College to consider such a major new venture. The college campus comprised a very large four-storey building together with a small disused school building called Woodlands. The student refectory – or canteen – occupied the whole of the fourth floor of the main building with wonderful views across London.

Immediately on her arrival at the college Ulla had convinced herself that the fourth-floor refectory was the scene of various nefarious activities by the largely Asian student population who travelled to Acton from Southall to escape parental oversight. Her solution was to close the fourth-floor refectory and to open a facility she called the 'Garden Cafeteria' on the ground floor of the Woodlands building.

This had the additional advantage that she had decided that the Woodlands building would be the location for the Student Services Unit, new to Acton College but very close to Ulla's heart. However, it did not seem to be attractive to students. But with the Garden Cafeteria providing the only student canteen facility the Woodlands building would become better used, particularly as Ulla had closed and boarded up the hitherto busy Reception office on the ground floor of the main building in order to ensure that Woodlands became the only information point for student enquiries.

There were two significant drawbacks in relation to the Garden Cafeteria. Firstly, the timescale from when Ulla took over the college was too tight to allow the new kitchen facilities to be installed by Ealing Council in time for the start of the new term. Consequently, for the first few weeks, whilst the new kitchen facilities were being constructed, the students were being offered only one choice for lunch – chilli con carne boiled up on camping stoves by increasingly resentful college canteen staff – the diet possibly also not being in line with the students' religious beliefs. And secondly, it immediately became clear that the Garden Cafeteria, attractively laid out though it was in cosy booths, was far too small for the student numbers which had previously been accommodated in the vast fourth floor refectory.

Ulla's solution was to deploy her small management team as dinner monitors, moving the students on as soon as it was seen that their plates were empty. The whole thing was utterly untenable and in due course I, together with another Vice Principal, decided to go to Ulla and tell her so. Although we were probably her two most loyal senior managers we were given short shrift.

After a moment's reflection she gave us a cold stare and said "There will be no return to the fourth floor". It was reminiscent of "The lady's not for turning" and I remember thinking "This will not end well". Meanwhile the vast fourth floor, with its magnificent views, was empty – ideal for the prestigious catering project which was now the focus of Ulla's ambitions.

When Ulla told the Hotel & Catering Training Board that she envisaged developing a large catering training facility to house Ciao Italia and others they said that, in that case, we needed to visit the USA where the best catering colleges were to be found. Within a few weeks Ulla and I found ourselves on a plane to New York, following an itinerary drawn up by the HCTB. We first went to the suspiciously labeled CIA which turned out to be the Culinary Institute of America, located in a huge mansion on the banks of the Hudson River in New York State.

We were treated like royalty. There were several restaurants, each specialising in the cuisine of a different nationality. The whole place ran like clockwork with students busily cooking, greeting customers, and serving food. In one we received our bill specifying how many calories we had consumed. Many of the customers were from the large number of high-profile businesses located nearby. We were tremendously impressed and took from it many lessons about providing a total catering experience for our students on our return. We visited many other establishments – one I recall was the CCI – the California Culinary Institute – but the CIA probably provided us with all we needed to know.

When we got back we first needed to recruit staff to plan the facilities and deliver the training. We were extremely fortunate to be able to engage Chris Witt, who not only turned out to be ideally suited to what we had in mind but also proved to be a lifelong friend – even being best man at my second wedding. He was appointed as Head of Catering in September 1987 and we fixed a time to meet up a few weeks later to familiarise Chris with Acton College and scope out the work needed.

We arranged to meet on Friday 16th October. This turned out to be the day following the prevous night's Great Storm of 1987 which devastated much of south east England. I remember driving across London, picking my way past fallen trees and other obstacles. Chris, on the other hand, travelling to Acton from the west, was largely unaware of these problems.

My young children, meanwhile, were recovering from the trauma of thinking we'd lost one of our two recently acquired kittens to the storm. One of them, Buttons, had sensibly stayed indoors but the other one, Johannes, had gone out through the cat-flap earlier. I'd just finished reassuring the children that Johannes would probably be found by a friendly neighbour when he slipped back in through the cat-flap and started hungrily eating from his tray.

Chris was brilliant at planning what was needed for the new catering training facility. He was assisted in this when Ulla insisted that he, together with his newly appointed Head of Department, Jean Carter, should themselves travel to the USA to repeat the visits to the catering colleges we had gone to a few months earlier. By the time he took up his post at Acton in January 1988 Chris had overseen the installation of state of the art training kitchens together with a so-called 'Training Wine Bar' on the fourth floor which we ran on a semicommercial basis and which became hugely popular with staff and college visitors. Chris even labeled up our own Acton College wine! Meanwhile the Ciao Italia discussions inched forward, of which more later.

I need also to mention our marketing efforts. We first needed to revamp the college's promotional material, particularly its annual prospectus which became our main vehicle for promoting the college as an attractive, welcoming and high quality institution. The college had also, enterprisingly, developed an overseas market, something completely new to me, recruiting students from the Far East, particularly Hong Kong, by working with an agency called Academic Asia and sending senior college managers to attend Education Fairs in Hong Kong itself.

Ulla was unimpressed by this practice and told me to join the Hong Kong visit team with a view to shutting the initiative down thereafter. I therefore made the journey and spent three or four days on the Hong Kong Polytechnic campus promoting Acton College courses to local youngsters and their parents. I was somewhat upstaged by the private college on the adjacent stand which permanently played a video showing the Queen on a tour of its campus. For some reason this attracted more interest than me and my new-look prospectus. However, we came away with a few more overseas students, all of whom paid full-cost fees and were therefore an additional income stream for the college.

Ulla was probably right in wanting to end the Hong Kong trips which were basically management 'jollies' so the one I went on was the last. However, there was clearly merit in the recruitment of overseas students and, building on the excellent work already done by the college, I used some of the overseas fee income to strengthen our links with Academic Asia, providing them with a proportion of the fee income in return for promoting Acton College through newspaper advertising and other promotional initiatives. The result was a steady increase in our overseas recruitment.

The overseas fee income went into my Marketing & Special Projects budget and its growth enabled me to fund various other money-making initiatives. One was the production of teaching materials for sale to other colleges. I was approached by two resourceful members of the engineering staff whose own teaching commitments had reduced and who had spotted that whenever new engineering courses were introduced nationally there was an initial dearth of appropriate teaching material which they felt they could provide. The result was a thriving micro-business publishing attractive teaching packs which we sold to colleges throughout the UK following adverts in various educational publications.

I had been at Acton for a couple of years when there was a dramatic development. Ulla called me into her office and said, "You're looking at the new Director of Education for Ealing". I was astounded. I said, "Good heavens. I'm very sorry you'll be leaving the college but congratulations. When do you start the new job?" "Monday" she replied. This meant an immediate requirement for a new temporary Acton College Principal and I knew that I would be well-placed to fill the position because my standing with the governors was high at the time. There was a short recruitment process and I was duly appointed.

I was well aware that mine was only a temporary appointment but there were a few things so urgent that I made some changes which I felt were necessary. The first of these was to rescind Ulla's 'No return to the fourth floor' edict. The Woodlands 'Garden Cafeteria' was still not working well and, despite the success of the fourth floor 'Training Wine Bar' there was still plenty of room on the huge fourth floor for a spacious student refectory. The move back was enormously popular and the integration of the student catering facilities with Chris's training arrangements, along the lines of the American experience, worked brilliantly. The other thing I did was to reopen the ground floor Reception office which also proved popular.

I applied for the permanent position but another candidate got it. However, the experience of the temporary post convinced me that a principalship was not beyond me. Before long Acton College was merged with other Ealing educational establishments to form a large Ealing Tertiary College. I would not have been in the running for its principalship but I learnt a lot about how to mount a successful appointment bid by studying how the successful candidate had gone about it. My chance came much quicker than I had anticipated.

The situation within the newly created Ealing Tertiary College was very fluid. No-one's job was safe and Chris Witt decided to leave for a head of department position in east London at Barking College of Technology. Soon afterwards I heard from him that the principalship of

Barking had been advertised. In view of the uncertain situation in Ealing I decided to apply. I did so, and overcame the first hurdle - I was shortlisted.

But hold on, I hear you ask – "What happened to Mr. Taverna and Ciao Italia?" There was, indeed, a further development in the tale. During the time when I was the temporary Principal of Acton College, and whilst Chris was still there, we received a phone call from Mr. Taverna. "We would like to book your fourth floor Boardroom and Wine Bar for a Ciao Italia afternoon event" he said. "That's great" I said, "No problem". He continued "Can you supply some pretty women to serve the drinks and canapés?" I'm afraid not", I replied "That wouldn't comply with our Equal Opportunities commitments". "No problem" responded Mr. Taverna. "We'll bring our own pretty women".

On the appointed day Chris and I looked down in amazement from our fourth floor vantage point to the large car park below. A stream of expensive cars entered and from them emerged a procession of equally expensive women, dressed in fur coats and similar regalia, accompanied by men who would not have looked out of place in 1950's gangster movies.

After socialising for a while in the Wine Bar, picking at the food and drink offered - yes - by the pretty women who had somehow materialised, they made their way into the Boardroom, conversing all the time in Italian. Once seated round the huge oval table which comprised the Boardroom furniture, they listened as Mr. Taverna regaled them with the proposal that the college's fourth floor should now become the new Italian catering school in England, closing down the small one currently based in Clerkenwell.

At the end of his speech he asked for approval from the assembled multitude. "Pizza Express, do you agree?" he asked. "Si" came the enthusiastic response. "Pizza Hut?" "Si". And so it went on. The only problem was that I had gathered, from the bits of Mr. Taverna's presentation which were in English, that he expected to purchase the college's fourth floor on a permanent basis. This was something of a problem. Firstly, the college was not mine to sell, being at that time firmly in the ownership of Ealing Council. Secondly, the recently appointed Principal was due to take up her post within the next few weeks and would not be too pleased to find that I had sold off a quarter of her new college.

There was only one solution which sprang into my disoriented mind. I invented an absurdly large sum of money and announced it as the purchase price. From around the room there was outrage and spluttering along the lines of "You gotta be joking. You brought us here under false pretences". Given the make-up of the assemblage I thought that my short but eventful life was nearing an abrupt end. However, with much loud grumbling the room emptied, the cars filed out of the car park and Chris and I breathed a sigh of relief at our narrow escape. For some reason we never heard from Mr. Taverna again, though Chris subsequently reported that he heard of him from time to time, touting the same proposal around other colleges.

With this excellent achievement behind me I set off with quiet confidence for my interview at Barking College of Technology.

Chapter 12

Barking College

I got the job and as soon as I walked into Barking College of Technology it felt as though I had come home. I became the principal in January 1992 and by the time I left nearly seventeen years later in August 2008 I had grown to love the place.

It's worth saying something about the borough of Barking and Dagenham. In 1992 when I got there it was described as 'mono-cultural', meaning totally white working class. In subsequent years the demography changed and from around 2000 the borough rapidly became more multi-cultural with low property prices making it a magnet for new arrivals.

The local council – the London Borough of Barking & Dagenham (LBBD) – was dominated by the Labour Party and was strongly committed to driving up local educational standards. The best example of this was when a superb headteacher – Paul Grant – took over a failing school – Robert Clack – and transformed it within a few years to become highly successful in every respect. Paul eventually received a knighthood in consequence – thoroughly deserved in my view. The council felt that having addressed the issues in their secondary schools it was time to focus on the Further Education college.

Barking College of Technology looked and felt

somewhat old-fashioned, characterised by a rather drab, uninviting entrance foyer and a number of old prefab-style workshops for the practical courses in which the college specialised. A recent 'Management Audit' conducted by Barking Council had concluded that there were many failings, particularly a dysfunctional management system, an absence of student support and the lack of a curriculum plan. I decided to use the time between getting the job and taking up the post to talk to as many people as possible – governors, staff, trade unionists and students – in order to prepare an initial plan of action and develop a sense of momentum.

On my first day in post I arrived at around 5am in order to be there when the first staff arrived – premises staff and cleaners – to meet them and introduce myself. I continued this as successive waves of staff arrived – maybe 150 in all – then made sure that arrangements were in place for a mass meeting of everyone in the large college refectory at around 10am.

At the meeting I outlined the programme of work I envisaged, central to which was a thorough-going reorganisation in which the numerous existing Departments would be replaced by fewer, larger, Faculties overseeing a number of 'Schools of Study' which would be the key providers of high-quality curriculum delivery.

Everything in the college was to be team-based. There would be a single 'Strategic Management Team' (SMT) to include Faculty Directors as well as other senior managers. The SMT would thus oversee all aspects of college life. Crucially the whole reorganisation plan would be subject to a time-limited consultation process beginning with the submission of initial ideas from all staff groups and ending with approval by the college Governing Body before implementation in September 1992.

Other priorities included ensuring that the college was ready for a government initiative of enormous importance, called 'Incorporation', which would remove colleges from local authority control and make them self-governing institutions from 1st April 1993. I also mentioned that I would be proposing changing the college name to 'Barking College' as it was now offering much more than 'Technology', and that I wanted an overhaul of the college's corporate image, with a new logo and suite of promotional material. I also wanted a new look entrance to the college, with a large open counter in front of a student services team.

On top of all this Barking Council had begun a new building programme at the college by digging out the foundations for what they called 'D' Block to provide teaching accommodation for a large number of our students. This was because when LBBD found out that the government planned to remove all existing college premises from local authority control and transfer them to the colleges they rushed through a proposal to close three of Barking College's outlying sites housing Art & Design, Business Studies and Brickwork in order to acquire the land themselves. In return they agreed to build 'D' Block as well as an adjacent 'E' Block housing a Brickwork workshop on the college's remaining Dagenham Road site. We therefore needed to plan the transfer of everything from the three outlying sites to the new building.

I ended my address by saying "We will do all this by the end of the summer term". This was greeted by laughter and gasps of disbelief. In the event nearly everything was achieved in line with this demanding schedule.

Key to the success of the college from the very beginning was the cohesion and commitment of the Strategic Management Team. I assembled, largely from existing senior staff, those that I felt could take the college forward. The SMT at the start of the 1992 autumn term numbered eight including myself. It comprised three outstanding Faculty Directors who would oversee the Schools of Study – Bert Furze (Technology), Bill Lobley (Business Studies) and Jill Jordan (Academic & Social Studies) – together with two colleagues from the previous College Management Team – John Sibley (Vice Principal, Finance & Estates) and Joanne Dean (Director of Personnel & Legal Services and Clerk to the Corporation). The two other Directors were Chris Witt (Marketing & Special Projects) and David Brunyee (Client Services).

We were joined before long by Steve Grix as Director of Curriculum Planning & Quality Assurance. Steve had previously been an education inspector with Barking Council and he proved invaluable in preparing the college for subsequent external inspections before going on to enjoy an outstanding career, next as a sixth-form college principal, followed by Director of Education at Tower Hamlets then Principal of MidKent College where he had begun his working life as a brickwork apprentice.

At an early stage I decided to take the SMT to the college's outward bound centre at Blaenavon in Wales for a gruelling week of team building to include hiking, pot-holing and strategic planning. This created some initial unease amongst the team members but seemed to serve its purpose by bringing us together and letting us get to know each other. Chris Witt and Joanne Dean came through with flying colours by being the only ones to complete the entire arduous pot-holing route, emerging from cracks in the rocks which looked far too narrow to squeeze through.

There were moments of fun beginning on the first night when the group was divided into two teams which competed to reach a map reference only to find it was a blacked-out pub. This was followed by elation when the lights came on and we were welcomed in by the event's organisers. The festivities were further enhanced when I noticed a piano and led the group in the raucous singing of some rock 'n roll favourites. A middle-aged courting couple sitting in a corner hoping we'd all go away asked who we were. Someone said we were from a college and they then asked who was the noisy person at the piano. When told it was the principal their astonishment was complete!

Whether or not the outward-bound experience contributed to bonding the team is unknown but in any event the SMT, changing its composition as circumstances required, was crucial to the college's success throughout my time there. The redoubtable Beattie Coe in due course replaced Bill Lobley following his early retirement due to illness. Jacqui Mace and then Sue Carroll replaced Steve Grix as Curriculum and Quality Director when he moved on, both of them bringing fresh energy and valuable insights.

The SMT developed the practice of meeting on Wednesday mornings to carry out the crucial task of preparing and implementing the college's Strategic Plan whilst each SMT member also managed on a day to day basis the middle management layer of Heads of School and key operational managers such as the premises and human resources managers.

All our senior managers had their own distinctive contributions to make to the subsequent success of the college. Chris Witt was an innovative, ever-cheerful and optimistic ambassador for the college which made him ideal in his marketing role and also in inspiring the hardworking Client Services team in offering a welcoming and supportive approach to potential and existing students when he took the team over following David Brunyee's departure.

Joanne Dean was methodical and painstaking, both in her Clerkship and Legal/HR roles, ensuring that we never fell foul of our legal or ethical obligations. She developed a comprehensive range of key college policies and was highly valued by the college's governing body – the 'Corporation' as it became known after Incorporation (see below). She established a worthy reputation well beyond the college in bodies such as the Association of Colleges.

I need to make particular mention of John Sibley, who, as a Vice Principal already in post when I took over, gave me invaluable support in overseeing the college's finances and its estates strategy. His role was fundamental to maintaining the financial health of the college and in beginning the transformation of the college's somewhat dilapidated estate.

When John Sibley decided to retire he pointedly remarked that we needed two senior managers to replace him – a Director of Finance to look after the money and a Director of Commercial & Estates Development, to continue the premises improvements. This latter role also encompassed running new income generating initiatives.

John's final appearance at the SMT was both a poignant and humorous one. He shared his recollections of all the other SMT members. Of me he said that I handled the vast amount of paperwork pouring into the college by delegating anything with words to my capable and resourceful Personal Assistant Sue Waidson whilst sending anything with numbers on it to him. He claimed that on one occasion he queried something I had sent to him, saying it had no numbers on it. When I showed him the numbers he said, "Ted, that's the date".

He gave everyone a leaving gift. Marketing Director Chris Witt, received a machine which allegedly printed five-pound notes in recognition of his habit of cheerfully overspending his budget. John's replacement as Director of Finance, Derek Camlin, kept our spending under control. He was in due course replaced by Ian Noutch who fitted in perfectly with our increasingly entrepreneurial style, epitomised by the other SMT appointment, Mike Rowton, of whom more later.

The support I received from the administrative staff of the college throughout my time there was tremendous. I should mention in particular my own Personal Assistants. My first PA, Jackie, played an important role in warning me whenever the 'old guard' was plotting to thwart the implementation of any of my bright ideas! The second one, Sue Waidson, who got me through the remainder of my years at the college, was an IT genius who compensated admirably for my failure to grasp new technology and made sure the office was properly prepared for the modern era.

Every SMT member had a Personal Assistant. Mine shared an office with other SMT PA's – notably Sue Pentecost (Finance & Estates) and Carole Piggott (Curriculum & Quality) – and together they formed a formidable and productive team.

The other people who made a huge – and unpaid – contribution to the success of the college were the members of the Governing Body – later renamed 'Corporation' after Incorporation (see below). There is not space here to provide a detailed account of everything they did on our behalf but I would like to mention the chairpersons who gave so freely of their time: -

Councillor Graham Bramley from LBBD was Chair of Governors when I arrived and continued in this role until Incorporation in 1993. He had been admirable in his wise stewardship of the college and remained on the reconfigured 'Corporation' thereafter.

Jim Scrimshaw, a senior manager with a nearby telecommunications company, joined us and took over as chair when the government made clear that it wanted colleges to be industry-led. His leadership was superb and in consequence he become widely know throughout the FE sector. He soon became Chair of the Association of Colleges which represented colleges throughout the country.

Elaine James took over after Jim left. She was a major force in the local voluntary sector, playing a key role in the Barking & Dagenham Disablement Association, a lively and entrepreneurial organisation. She helped the college orient itself on local voluntary groups to great mutual advantage. She, like Jim Scrimshaw before her, became recognised within the wider FE Sector and as a Chair of Corporation who was also a member of an ethnic minority group she had her own very special contribution to make.

As well as their hard work within the college we periodically held Corporation/SMT residentials outside to receive progress reports and develop strategy. I recall one such event in Rotherhithe at a humble religious venue we had booked to demonstrate that we were not spending college money extravagantly. The bedrooms were rather cell-like and we were summoned by a bell to a trestle table for communal meals. Soon after arrival one of the governors, rather large in stature, announced to the group, but for my special attention, that he could not get into his room. When I expressed surprise, remarking that it was the policy of the religious order to have no keys and therefore to have all rooms unlocked, he said, "No, it's not that. I physically can't get in – the room's too small". I concluded that he was exaggerating. However, for future residentials I reverted to the more traditional conference settings.

Incorporation

I have already mentioned a national development of great importance for all Further Education (FE) Colleges called 'Incorporation'. This stemmed from a decision by the Conservative government to take colleges out of local authority control and give them their independence from 1st April 1993. The whole FE Sector, as the totality of nearly 500 FE colleges became known, was to be run by a new body which proved to be extremely effective – the Further Education Funding Council (FEFC).

Incorporation was strongly welcomed by virtually all college principals and I myself was wholly in favour of colleges running their own affairs rather than having to get approval from local authorities for such things as funding, staffing and premises alterations. Colleges now found themselves being funded according to a strict funding formula based on their student numbers following which they had to manage everything within the funding thus generated. Some college principals buckled under this responsibility and had to be replaced. Most, however, thrived. We certainly did at Barking.

With the coming of Incorporation a previously marginal aspect of college work became crucially important. This was 'Management Information Systems' – MIS. We needed to count every student and allocate to them a weighting factor determined by the FEFC depending on what learning programme, or combination of learning programmes, they were engaged in. This was all fiendishly complicated and upon it depended the college income – and in our case (see 'Caseloading' below) our internal allocation of funds to all areas of college activity, crucially the Schools of Study.

We needed to appoint an MIS Manager capable of understanding the complexity of the data needed and able to develop the powerful IT systems needed to provide it. We could not have been more fortunate in our choice of MIS Manager. In a quiet, unassuming but extraordinarily efficient way Bharat Rathod arrived at the college and transformed how the place worked. Not only did he produce the sophisticated data required by the FEFC but he also provided real-time data for college managers which enabled them to fine-tune their learning programmes to maximise income and monitor student progress. Bharat had an encyclopedic grasp of FE learning programmes. So too did another of our managers – Mike Rowton.

Franchising

The FEFC used a crucial document 'Rules 101' produced by the Department for Education & Science (DES) listing all the courses for which they would provide funding. The list was enormous. John Sibley called me into his office one morning. He was with Mike Rowton who at the time was Head of the School of Construction Technicians. One of Mike's claims to fame was that in a previous life he had overseen the construction of one of the bridges over the nearby A13 road, something he never failed to mention whenever we drove under it. He has subsequently told me that he was ashamed of having been required to design such an ugly structure!

John had an anxious look on his face, which was not unusual. But there also seemed to be an underlying air of excitement. He said, "Mike has spotted something in the FEFC's funding guidance. It seems to provide an opportunity to increase our funding but I'm not sure it's allowed". Thus began another initiative of huge importance for the college – something in which we were one of the first in the field. It was called Franchising.

The guidance seemed to allow colleges to claim funding for courses which they didn't deliver themselves by partnering with outside organisations which would themselves deliver the training. Mike was a keen yachtsman and suggested that by partnering with sailing schools we could get them to expand their training activities and register the new students as Barking College students, attracting FEFC funding and splitting the income between us. Clearly, if this was deemed acceptable by the FEFC we could apply the principle to other areas of training including upskilling commercial companies and community organisations.

Mike wrote to the FEFC explaining clearly what we were proposing and asking for approval. He received a reply from the FEFC Assistant Director of Curriculum, Geoff Daniels, just before Christmas saying, "What you are proposing appears to be a form of Franchising or Outward Collaborative Provision. We would encourage you to expand your activities with commercial companies and other organisations". Mike has a recollection of me dancing round the room when I read the letter. The whoops of joy must have been heard far beyond the office and led to a whole new area of college activity.

We created a new Division of Commercial and Estates Development and Mike joined the SMT as its Director. There were thus two important areas under Mike's direction – the continuing development of college premises and the expansion of our franchising activities. The latter proved highly lucrative and I joined Mike and his enterprising bunch on several adventures in order to establish partnerships with as many organisations as possible.

An early initiative was to print off a list of the top 200 companies and get appointments to see their training managers. Among other things this led Mike and me to take a train journey to Leeds to see the Asda supermarket management with a view to getting their staff trained in customer care.

On the way there and back we treated our fellow passengers to lengthy expositions on the mutual benefits of working with Barking College. Mike is convinced that the female manager of an IT company got off the train before she reached her destination because she could stand my enthusiastic treatise no longer. Perhaps it was when she said, "I'm not interested" and I replied, "Well, you couldn't have understood it – let me go through it again" which resulted in her early departure.

Bit by bit our expertise and the client list of Mike's team developed and the outward-looking approach to partnership working spread to other aspects of college work. The need to ensure probity in these complex arrangements led Mike to develop a legally binding contract governing the relationship between Barking College and its partners. Mike prepared the initial draft then worked with our lawyers, Mills & Reeve, to finalise the document which in due course was adopted by the FEFC as its 'Model Contract' for colleges running franchising. We also created, within Mike's division, a number of posts to monitor the quality of training and the validity of student data being supplied by our partner organisations.

Nationally the impact of franchising was to greatly expand the amount of training being undertaken by companies and community organisations. It offered a real opportunity to upskill the nation. However the incoming 1997 Labour government abolished the FEFC and replaced it with a rather less effective 'Learning & Skills Council' (LSC) and, following active lobbying from a few influential colleges which disapproved of franchising, the practice fell out of favour.

In view of the complexity of the new demands facing colleges I had decided soon after Incorporation that I should have some kind of management training, so I booked myself onto an MBA course being run at the Further Education Staff College located at Coombe Lodge in Somerset. It was a residential course consisting of a series of one-week modules taken over two years. It was there, as mentioned earlier, that I met my second wife, Jennifer.

The course was solely for further education managers, most of whom were from the UK though there were also colleagues from Denmark. Jennifer was a head of department at Accrington & Rossendale College in Lancashire. I have to confess that I was the only participant on the MBA course who failed to complete it – I ended up not finishing my final assignment, largely, in my view, because I was increasingly busy by then as principal of a large fast-growing and successful college. However, what I learnt on the course including ideas from Jennifer's college proved hugely beneficial to Barking.

Caseloading

At Jennifer's college, Accrington & Rossendale, the Principal, Mike Austin, was a regular columnist in the Times Educational Supplement. As a contribution to a debate about controversial flexible new contracts for lecturing staff he developed a concept called 'Caseloading' which replaced 'teaching hours' (hours in the classroom) as a determinant of a lecturer's contractual obligation with 'caseload' which meant total student hours (i.e. teaching hours times student numbers). I got Jennifer to bring a small team to Barking to explain the concept.

In due course this idea became pivotal to managing Barking College and shaped everything we did throughout my time there. The vital step we took at Barking, uniquely as far as I know, was to link the FEFC's funding regime to the caseloading concept by allowing the Schools of Study to keep 50% of the money generated by their student numbers, the remainder being retained centrally for administration, support services and reserves. Schools were then free to deliver the curriculum in any way they liked within specified quality guidelines such as taught hours required per course. This transferred financial power to the Schools of Study, particularly the Heads of School, and they responded superbly, striving to maximize overall student numbers whilst matching the income generated to expenditure on staff salaries.

The Schools of Study, created as part of the original reorganisation, proved to be ideally suited to the caseloading approach. As previously noted they were the means by which the college courses were delivered.

The appointment of first-rate Heads of School, initially from amongst the college staff, had been an important early task for the college. There were about seventeen Schools of Study including such specialisms as Performing Arts, Photography, Construction and Leisure & Tourism. All the resources of the college were brought to bear to provide every School of Study with what it needed in staffing, accommodation and teaching resources to deliver courses of the highest possible quality – but cost effectively – and caseloading provided the key.

One of the biggest successes was the School of Construction Crafts. Its Head of School was an excellent brickwork lecturer named Andrew Brader. I first came across Andrew just after I became Principal. He was teaching his brickwork students in appalling conditions at an outlying college site called Faircross. However, the students were all working hard and were clearly highly motivated. It was evident to me, both by observing his teaching and from his performance during the interviews for the Head of School post, that Andrew had great potential.

When he got the job the School was in a difficult financial situation. It had relatively few students, so under the new FEFC funding regime it generated limited income, but there were a lot of staff and the income was not sufficient to pay their wages. They were also highly unionised and openly antagonistic to 'management', which was true of many of the lecturing staff when I first joined the college.

I clearly remember my first encounter with the Construction staff. Andrew had called them together to explain the situation and he and I did a double-act, sitting with them round a table in one of the classrooms. We got the message across. The only way we could balance the books was by recruiting more students or by cutting staff numbers, using funds for voluntary redundancy being made available under an FEFC 'restructuring' fund. In the event we did both. Some staff left but the number of students mushroomed until, by the time Andrew and I left Barking, we had one of the biggest Construction training operations in London.

All the Schools of Study were remarkable in their different ways. The Head of Performing Arts, John McDermott, ran his team so effectively that in subsequent external inspections his courses were never judged less than 'Outstanding'. Long before I arrived at the college John had already taught such impressive performers as Idris Elba and Marianne Jean-Baptiste, the first black actress to be nominated for an Oscar in Mike Leigh's film "Secrets & Lies".

In the School of Photography the Head of School, Ed Kinge, recruited a delightful student, Penny Lancaster, who opted to undertake a student assignment by taking photos of Rod Stewart. Having done so she then went on to marry him! For every School of Study there would be great tales to tell but unfortunately the telling would double the size of this book.

College accommodation

As well as ending up with one of the largest Construction training facilities anywhere we also had some of the best Construction workshops in the country. It was part of the FEFC's remit to deliver world-class

Further Education in world-class buildings, replacing the existing tired old college premises with impressive new architect-designed structures housing high quality classrooms, learning centres and workshops. As ever, the FEFC was as good as its word, engaging outstanding construction specialists to work with colleges in upgrading their estates to very high standards. Again, everything depended on student numbers with colleges needing to produce robust forecasts of planned growth in order to justify FEFC investment on new buildings, usually to be supplemented by contributions from colleges' own financial reserves.

Barking College was ideally placed to become an attractive and well-designed estate. The college footprint was unusually large, occupying several acres adjacent to a country park on one side and low-level housing on the other. However, we were considerably disadvantaged by Barking Council's rushed design for the large three-storey 'D' Block which had to house hundreds of our students following their ejection from the three outlying sites taken over by the Council prior to Incorporation. 'D' Block was cheaply built and from the beginning we disliked its thin walls and fragile construction. Soon after Incorporation we paid for a thoroughgoing professional survey which revealed some startling flaws.

By far the worst thing we discovered was that there were serious fire safety concerns. Two key decisions followed. Firstly, we instituted immediate additional fire safety precautions and commissioned major improvements including reinforcing the structure and creating additional staircases for emergency evacuation purposes. Secondly, to recoup the considerable costs we engaged a prestigious law firm, Mills & Reeve, to sue the original builders, which resulted in a £1.5 million settlement. The relationship with Mills & Reeve, managed largely through our Director of Personnel & Legal Services, Joanne Dean, endured thereafter, proving invaluable in ensuring that the college remained legally secure in the many ventures in which we became engaged.

In due course we constructed a superb new building which provided linkage between the existing buildings at the two ends of our long site. We named this impressive addition to our estate 'The Bramley Building' in honour of the Barking & Dagenham Council Member, Graham Bramley, who had been a long-serving Chair of Governors before Incorporation. The naming of the building was also in recognition of the service of his wife, Sue Bramley, herself a local councillor who had sadly died shortly beforehand, having made a major contribution to the community, particularly through her championing of childcare provision.

In the new building we located our excellent Construction workshops and our Art & Design studios as well as a spacious concourse area which became a focal point for college events of all kinds. On one occasion many of us gathered to watch a World Cup football match on TV. I was waving a temporary aerial about trying to get a decent picture, which led Andrew Brader to drily remark that we hadn't had long to prepare for the match! I remember with great affection my own uproarious leaving 'do' which brought together all the staff, the governors, some students and many visitors. There was food, drink and music – we got a staff rock band together which gave me a chance to inflict some songs on the assembled masses – I enjoyed attempting a version of Bruce Springsteen's 'Hungry Heart' which went down well – at least with me.

Other big improvements to our learning facilities came about as a result of our active engagement with developments within our locality. One arose from our close involvement with the Ford Motor Company located on its historic Dagenham estate. From early in 2000 there had been proposals from the London Development Agency, in partnership with Fords, to undertake a massive redevelopment of Dagenham's riverside, using land which Ford would relinquish in line with its long-term corporate planning. One element of the redevelopment plan was the creation of something designated as a 'Learning Centre'.

When I spotted this I made sure that I became part of the planning process and joined the Board overseeing the overall regeneration project. The idea of a Learning Centre developed into a plan for a so-called Centre for Engineering & Manufacturing Excellence (CEME). I made clear that the two local Further Education colleges – Barking and Havering – which already did the training for Ford's apprentices – could provide students and a funding stream which could make CEME financially viable.

This led to the two colleges becoming important elements in the planning of CEME. Both I and the Havering College Principal, Noel Otley, joined the CEME Board and agreed to contribute £1 million each to the capital costs. However, the project was completely Ford-driven. I could not have been more impressed by the way in which the Ford team brought an unswerving focus to getting the job done. They got the architects to design a world-class futuristic building, they ensured that the builders stuck to deadlines and budgets and they got the place equipped, staffed and ready to run by September 2004. I also recall drinking endless cups of coffee during the planning meetings – and hearing the Board chairman repeatedly saying, whenever anyone suggested doing anything differently – "we've got a plan – stick to it!"

The two colleges felt that for CEME purposes they should present a single image when recruiting students so we badged ourselves as 'Thames Gateway College'. It suited one of Barking's top managers, Bert Furze, to transfer to CEME. This left a vacancy within our SMT which was filled in due course by the equally able Andrew Brader who took on the role of Director of the Faculty of Art, Design & Technology (ADT). When CEME became operational we were able to base two of our Schools of Study there – the School of Mechanical Engineering and the School of Motor Vehicle Engineering. The students thus found themselves in facilities unequalled anywhere in the country.

Another step change to our learning facilities arose from our strong links with the local council. I have already mentioned our excellent School of Performing Arts which nurtured so many performers under the dedicated leadership of its Head of School, John McDermott. John and I had long had the ambition to create improved facilities for the Performing Arts students and an opportunity arose to do this some miles from the college in the heart of Barking town centre. I was strongly influenced in this by Jennifer's experiences at Oldham College which had taken over the Grange Arts Centre and made it accessible to the local community for theatrical performances.

Barking & Dagenham Council, through an imaginative council officer named Jeremy Grint, made an old assembly hall named the Broadway Theatre available and the college enthusiastically entered into a partnership to turn it into a proper performance venue, with the college occupying the basement area with dance studios, rehearsal rooms and music technology facilities.

The Broadway Theatre was remodeled by Tim Foster Architects in 2006 with an attractive foyer, box office and an auditorium seating 341. From then on it offered a wide range of commercial performances as well as student productions. It is still operating as a superb learning environment for students as well as providing a rich programme of music, dance and drama for local residents.

Two other significant initiatives involving partnership with Barking Council are worth mentioning. We found that we could work with local libraries to install computers and carry out IT training for local people, benefitting the whole community in what we called 'Learning Villages'. By 2005-06 we were operating at several locations and enrolling 3,000 learners a year.

At one stage we were contemplating locating an entire college in Barking Town Centre. The Council had plans of their own which conflicted with this ambition but we nevertheless managed to work with them in contributing towards the capital costs of an impressive 'Barking Learning Centre' which was a 'one stop shop' for Council services, library services and learning programmes delivered by the college. Since then this approach has been adopted with local variants by local authorities throughout the country.

Some turbulent times

During the whole of my time at Barking College it was a focal point for opposition to racism. We were therefore alarmed when in May 2006 twelve members of the racist British National Party (BNP) were elected onto Barking and Dagenham Council. I was one of the speakers at the street demonstrations organised to oppose the BNP by Unite Against Fascism and I was able to use the college to host Love Music Hate Racism (LMHR) events to promote anti-racism through music.

Robert Bailey, the local BNP leader, visited the college to tell me there would be trouble if we continued to support these events. He left saying, "You have been warned", a remark which led to a front page headline in the local 'Recorder' newspaper reading 'BNP man threatens college'. In the 2010 elections all twelve BNP Councillors lost their seats.

The college got on TV a few times. I remember when the Ford Motor Company announced it was stopping car production in Dagenham. News reporters were on the lookout for quotes bemoaning the disastrous impact on the local economy. When Evan Davis (now of 'Dragon's Den' and Radio 4's 'PM' fame) arrived at the college to do an interview for Panorama his first question to me, as

Principal, was, 'Well, this is terrible news, isn't it?" I said, "It's a setback but we'll get over it".

"What do you mean'" he said. "Where will these guys get a job?" I said, "We're talking about London – one of the most dynamic cities in Europe – there are jobs everywhere!" He replied, " 'What about the guys working on the assembly lines? They're not IT specialists or financial wheeler dealers, what jobs can they do?" I said, "Well, for example, what about plumbing? Have you tried to get a plumber recently?" He said, "What do you mean? That they could all do plumbing?" I said. "We're crying out for plumbers. But there are skills shortages covering the whole range of Construction skills and here at the college we've got the largest Construction training facility in London".

As soon as we stopped filming, one of the camera crew sidled up to me and said, "Look, I really need a plumber and can't find one – do you know where can I get one?" That autumn there were queues round the block to join our plumbing courses – and I gather that was happening nationally. I wouldn't want to claim all the credit – but who knows?

By the time I left Barking College in summer 2008 we'd somehow managed to house our students in first-class accommodation, we'd expanded enormously our stu-dent numbers – it peaked at around 30,000 a year in-cluding all the enrolments with partner organisations – and we'd made a significant contribution to the regener-ation of Barking & Dagenham and its environs. We also had £10 million in the bank – a rare achievement among FE colleges. Not a bad record all in all.

Chapter 13

The Rolex Murder

One of Mike Rowton's many entrepreneurial initiatives at Barking College had a memorable outcome. In 1997 Mike was running a one-day VHF radio course for yachtsmen when one of the students called Ron Platt mentioned to Mike that he was a qualified counsellor and a partner in his own firm, a counselling practice that had contracts with the Home Office and various police forces, amongst other organisations. Ron said he was interested in teaching counselling skills. After getting the approval of the appropriate awarding body Mike set up a course and Ron began teaching on it. We got to know him as an able and popular colleague, well liked by his students.

Unfortunately, at the time the real Ron Platt had been dead for a year, his body fished out of the sea six miles off the coast of Devon when it became caught in the net of the Brixham trawler Malkerry on 28th July 1996. The only clue to the identity of the corpse was a 25-year-old Rolex Oyster watch attached to the right wrist.

One day, a few months after the start of the Counselling Skills course, Mike received a phone call from one of the other partners in the practice who said that the person we knew as Ron Platt had been arrested for murdering the real Ron Platt and that police searches of his home and office had revealed gold ingots, large amounts of cash and a number of forged passports.

After going through the meticulous service records of the Rolex company the police had been able to identify the murder victim as 51-year old former soldier Ronald Platt and to establish that he had used an address in Essex. Whilst visiting the property they were astonished to be told by a neighbour that Ron Platt was still living there.

They put the place under surveillance and after a painstaking investigation it emerged that the real identity of the amiable college lecturer was Canada's most wanted criminal, businessman Albert Walker, who had fled across the Atlantic to London with his 15-year-old daughter in December 1990 following the alleged theft of nearly £3 million from his financial services business.

On arrival in the UK he chose the identity of one of his Canadian clients – David Davies – to use as his own. Later, in Harrogate, he befriended the former soldier and now TV repairman Ronald Platt and his girlfriend, using them to set up a company to launder cash. When they had served their purpose, Walker paid for them to start a new life in Canada and assumed Ron Platt's name as his second alias. But when a disillusioned and jobless Mr Platt returned to Britain in 1995 he became a threat to Walker's security and freedom.

In July the following year Walker took Mr Platt out on his 24ft yacht Lady Jane, which he kept moored at Dittisham in the River Dart, knocked him unconscious with a blow to the back of his head and threw him into the sea, with a 10lb anchor tucked into his trouser belt.

The students in the counselling skills class could not believe it when told that their beloved lecturer would not be available to teach them one evening because he had been arrested for murder. By then 52, he was jailed for life at Exeter Crown Court in 1998 after being found guilty. He was transferred back to Canada to see out his sentence in 2005. There have been at least two books and three TV documentaries about this remarkable case.

Chapter 14

Daggers v Addicks – divided loyalties

A chapter of this book covers my time at Barking College. Elsewhere I have mentioned my support for Charlton Athletic Football Club. A memorable occasion in 2001 unexpectedly brought these two aspects of my life together.

The event was a clash between my two favourite football teams. Although I was a season ticket holder with Charlton Athletic (then in the Premiership) I had also established a close relationship with Dagenham & Redbridge Football Club (then in the lowly Football Conference) because Barking College was sponsoring the club to the mutual benefit of both partners.

When Dagenham (the Daggers) drew Charlton (the Addicks) in the third round of the FA Cup I faced a conflict of loyalties. I chose Charlton but was aware of the huge interest in the forthcoming game at Barking College and throughout the Dagenham area. On Saturday 6th January, the massed ranks of Daggers' supporters filled the away section of Charlton's ground (the Valley) – and even infiltrated the home fans' area. The noise from the Daggers' supporters totally overwhelmed the chanting of the home fans.

The Daggers' players dominated the game and to chants of, 'Score in a minute, we're gonna score in a minute' they soon went one-nil up. There was rapturous applause. It looked as though they were going to pull off a major cup upset till Charlton's John Salako snatched a flukey last-minute equaliser.

The replay was scheduled for an evening ten days later and Sky TV arranged to cover the event, agreeing to pay £250,000 for the privilege – an absolute fortune for the cash-strapped Dagenham club. The Daggers' business manager, Steve Thompson, was overjoyed and somehow pulled together £25,000 to build a temporary press box to house the Sky commentators. The excitement was palpable and I popped down to the ground several times to share the anticipatory mood.

Essex Radio got to hear of my split loyalties and decided the situation warranted an item on their breakfast show on the day of the match. It was arranged that I would meet their news team at 6.30am in the Daggers' car park. When I arrived, on one of the coldest mornings of the year, there was a single Essex Radio reporter in an outside broadcast vehicle. I joined him in the back of the van and he said, "We'll go live on air immediately after the 7am news. I'll explain the situation then hand over to you. Unfortunately, I've got a slight problem. My aerial keeps slipping down so I'll have to nip out from time to time to pump it up".

7am arrived. I listened to the news, rehearsing in my head what I was about to say. The reporter waited for his moment then spoke into the microphone. "I'm here in the car park of Dagenham & Redbridge Football Club. At present it's deserted but tonight it will be packed with excited fans arriving for a crucial FA Cup replay against the Premiership team, Charlton Athletic. Someone who has a special interest in the game is Barking College

Principal, Ted Parker." He broke off and turned to me to say, "Oh blast – my aerial's gone down". He dashed outside as the Essex Radio announcer said, "Well we seem to have lost contact with Dagenham so let's go on to the next item".

Despite desultory attempts to re-establish contact that was the end of my sports radio career. However, far worse was to come. I went on to the college to catch up with paperwork but with the forthcoming evening match very much in mind. At around lunchtime I got a phone call from the Daggers' ground. The referee had turned up and declared that it was unsafe to play because of a frozen pitch. This news produced horror among the Daggers' staff. Phone calls to Sky TV confirmed that their payment would only be made if the match took place. Desperate attempts were made to warm up the pitch. Steve Thompson even walked around with a hairdryer but to no avail. The full consequences sunk in. Not only the loss of the £250,000 windfall but also the waste of the £25,000 spent on the press box.

At first there was a hope that Sky might cover the re-scheduled match but it was not to be. The date was fixed for Saturday 27th January and Sky were not able to cover 3pm Saturday fixtures. The game duly took place with the Daggers hoping that a victory could continue their Cup run and earn them some more money. However, on a pitch more reminiscent of a ploughed field than the pristine turf back at Charlton, a hard-fought battle ended with a one-nil victory for Charlton and the end of the Daggers' 2001 FA Cup dream.

But I'm pleased to say the story does not end there. Both

Barking College and Charlton Athletic retained considerable affection for the Dagenham team and did what they could to support them in various ways. The college increased its sponsorship, benefitting from the creation of a 'Barking College Family Stand' which afforded continuing publicity for the college in return for an annual payment which was welcomed by the club whilst being affordable by the college. We also established a Computer Learning Centre in a hut in the club's car park which provided local people with access to computer training whilst earning income for the college and rent for the club.

Among my many fond memories of the Daggers are the generous buffets provided in the club lounge whenever we had a Barking College sponsored match. You could have as much pie and mash as you could eat. Great times!

Chapter 15

Retirement

I retired in August 2008. The year had begun interestingly. On Friday 25th January the Barking College Governing Body met to select a new principal to replace me when I left. It was not appropriate for me, as the existing postholder, to be involved in the selection process but I was obviously interested in the outcome.

Anticipating a decision by late afternoon I had arranged to see a film with Jennifer that evening at the Greenwich Picture House. In the event the selection took longer and we ended up going to a late screening and then having a meal.

When I went to bed my arm felt uncomfortably numb. When I woke up the next morning I had some chest pains and found it difficult to breathe. It struck me that I might be having a heart attack. I therefore took the sensible decision to have a shower in case I ended up in hospital. I meanwhile asked Jennifer to phone up for medical advice, outlining my symptoms. I heard her shout out to me that the advice was to call an ambulance. By now in mid-shower I replied that it would be a good idea. She then said anxiously, "They're coming now and want me to leave the front door open. For heaven's sake get out of the shower."

I did so, and immediately heard heavy footsteps on

the stairs. I pulled on a tee shirt as Jennifer whispered, "Quick, lie on the bed and look ill". An amiable medic appeared, lugging an oxygen tank onto the bed and said, "Here, take a whiff of this". Within seconds there were more footsteps and two attractive young female paramedics joined us. I think my heart might have skipped a further beat at the sight. The first guy said, "I'm Charlie and these are my Angels".

One of them pulled up my tee shirt and attached some probes to my chest. She looked at some readings then said, "Look, I don't want you to get too alarmed". "I know," I said, "I'm having a heart attack". "Yes" she said. Behind her I could see Jennifer, who wilted on hearing the diagnosis, and the first guy offered her some oxygen.

They said, "We're taking you straight to hospital". "OK" I said, and started to get up. "No" they all shouted in unison. "Get on the stretcher". As I was being loaded into the ambulance my neighbour Alan Ring materialised and, having had a heart attack himself a few months earlier, was able to dispense some helpful medical advice for which I'm sure they were very grateful.

The paramedics then 'blue-lighted' me and Jennifer to King's College Hospital and within minutes I was watching a screen whilst an excellent young surgeon showed me that there was a dangerous narrowing of an artery in an awkward place. He explained that without treatment there would be a catastrophic worsening in 24 to 48 hours and that "60% don't make it". I needed to have a stent injected into my groin. It would then be moved up to my heart to open up the narrowed artery to keep the blood supply flowing.

I watched the screen with the surgeon and his team as they carried out this intricate procedure and was absolutely in awe of the calmness and professionalism they displayed throughout. They brought Jennifer up to date with what had happened and I was transferred to a ward where the superb level of care continued until I was discharged after a few days. I received a huge number of cards from work wishing me well and I was able to return to the college in good spirits a month later.

The new principal was joining the college after Easter and I was therefore able to spend three months introducing her to staff and external partners before I left in August. I had a memorable lunchtime leaving do in which all the staff and many of the students took part together with some of my friends and family.

I then received a completely unexpected honour from the University of East London (UEL) which awarded me an Honorary Doctorate in Education to recognise my contribution to education in the East London area. The Awards Ceremony took place in the Barbican Conference Centre at the same time as a graduation ceremony for a cohort of UEL's Technology students. In my acceptance speech I paid my own tribute to their achievements.

I was surprised to find that another of the five or so people receiving honorary awards was none other than Bob Geldof who was receiving an Honorary Doctorate in Music. I was seated next to him on the stage. He whispered to me as one by one the hundreds of granduands stepped up to receive their certificates. "This is wonderful," he said "but such a pity they are all taking these skills abroad".

I realised that Bob, perhaps unfamiliar with the demography of east London, thought that the students, drawn largely from ethnic minority groups, were from overseas. I whispered back, "I think they're mainly local". "Mainly local?" he repeated "Surely not". "Well, we'd need to check with the Vice Chancellor" I said, "but I think so". The Vice Chancellor was sitting on my other side and Bob leaned across. "Are these students mainly from overseas?" he asked. She looked surprised and replied, "Well, we've got some international students but they're mostly local".

Bob sat deep in thought. When it was his turn to make an acceptance speech he did it brilliantly. He began with some recollections I'd heard him recount before when he'd addressed an education conference a year or two earlier. He spoke about his somewhat bleak early years in Ireland which were transformed when he heard the intermittent transmissions of Radio Luxemburg broadcasting American rock 'n roll. It had been the same for me – heavenly forbidden music! For Bob it paved the way for a life in rock music and, along the way, the extraordinary triumph of Live Aid from Wembley.

He then turned to the matter in hand, the graduation of the UEL students. "Today" he said, "has been a wonderful experience for me. I've seen the future of London parading before me". The applause from the students and their proud parents was ecstatic. I silently congratulated myself on having given him a vital clue! Afterwards the honorary awardees and their guests got together for lunch. Bob had brought some members of his band along so Jennifer was able to enjoy a memorable conversation with a Boom Town Rat.

Soon after my retirement I was approached by Carl Blackburn, the Chief Executive of the Barking & Dagenham Council for Voluntary Service (CVS) who asked me whether I would be prepared to be the CVS chairperson in a voluntary capacity. I said I would be delighted and, although it meant a lot of travelling from home, I spent three fascinating years in the role. The CVS was an umbrella organisation overseeing dozens of local voluntary and community groups of which I had been largely unaware.

Some of the liveliest groups were those bringing together residents from different ethnic or linguistic backgrounds, such as refugees from war-torn Kosovo or Portuguese speakers, not only from mainland Portugal but also from its former African colonies. There was a highly entrepreneurial organization called the Barking & Dagenham Disablement Association which, as well as lobbying for improvements for people with disabilities, ran various moneymaking schemes such as IT training. Another interesting group comprised a number of allotment-holders who had banded together to build a clubhouse and create a wonderland of colour and water features in an area surrounded by Barking & Dagenham council houses.

Altogether I was enormously impressed by the amount of voluntary activity which was going on, making the area a better place in which to live. I got to know the groups by writing articles about one or other of them every fortnight for the Council's free newspaper. Every so often we would get everyone together for a conference, an awards event or some entertainment – perhaps a dance show by one or more of the national organisations.

A year after I left Barking College Jennifer took early retirement and we were able to take part in some voluntary activities together. By far the most time-consuming of these involved the local Bob Hope Theatre (BHT), so named because Bob Hope had spent his early years in Eltham before going as a young child to the USA where he became one of that country's most successful entertainers. He returned on a sentimental journey to Eltham in later life and donated money to the Eltham Little Theatre which decided to adopt his name.

The connection outlived Bob's death. Following several years during which Jennifer made her mark as a performer and director she became the theatre's Chairperson and built on an existing relationship with the Bob & Dolores Hope Foundation in America, nurtured over many decades by a BHT stalwart, Jim Shepherd. This enabled the theatre to secure funding from the Foundation for a major new building project which contributed to making the place the best-equipped amateur theatre in South London. Bob's daughter, Linda, and other members of the Foundation came to England in 2018 for an event to mark the theatre's re-launch after its extensive refurbishment.

My own involvement in the theatre was more modest

though quite demanding, including a stint as a member of the theatre's Board of Management, working as a front of house volunteer for the many theatrical and musical performances and running a monthly Folk & Blues evening in the theatre bar.

This last commitment was particularly fulfilling, allowing me to perform music to intimate and responsive audiences in an agreeable alcohol-fuelled setting. My speciality was a kind of 'swamp rock' - Green River by Creedence Clearwater Revival would be an example - accompanying myself with what I hoped sounded like a 'deep south' whining from my electric guitar. Luckily the voice still seemed to be holding out.

An especially enjoyable holiday at the time involved a trip to some famous music venues in America's southern states. We visited the Tupelo Hardware Store where Elvis got his first guitar. I persuaded one of the staff to lend me a guitar and inflicted my own version of 'That's Alright Mama' on the shoppers! The Folk & Blues evenings also enabled me to develop an enjoyable and productive musical partnership with someone called Pat Adams who became a great friend of Jennifer and myself. She was a singer with lots of experience in local theatres and in time we developed an extensive and wide-ranging repertoire.

At Jennifer's suggestion I also joined Rock Choir, a national organisation with nearly 30,000 singers, all learning identical songs every week so they could get together for various charity and community performances. My own local Rock Choir in Bexleyheath had about 200 members meeting in two separate rehearsal groups, and for ten years this has been a hugely enjoyable part of my life. Rock Choir even got together for huge national choral events in places such as Wembley Arena. It opened 'Proms in the Park' in Hyde Park on a couple of occasions.

The Rock Choir experience was made particularly enjoyable as a result of the talent and enthusiasm of the local Rock Choir leader, Michael Fricker. He never failed to enthuse and inspire the choir and even took us on tour abroad – to his home country of Switzerland where we performed in a music festival and at a church service – and later to France where we sang first at Disneyland and then in a park outside Notre Dame in Paris.

I found a most productive way of bringing together our local Rock Choir and the Bob Hope Theatre. Jennifer's plays were superb productions, often with musical elements. For example, in 'Blood Wedding' I provided a flamenco guitar backing, accompanied by a local world-class violinist called Yana Burova. In due course I found that if I advertised these productions to the Rock Choir members there was great interest.

The response was such that, for one performance, we were able to fill the whole 190-seat theatre almost entirely with Rock Choir members. We then combined this with an after-show visit to the local pub, the White Hart,then run by our good friends Dave and Simon Hinchley-Robson. Rock Choir members could thus enjoy a theatrical production together then pack out the pub for a superb buffet, laid on by the White Hart staff, before delivering a raucous Rock Choir performance much appreciated by the pub's regulars. Everyone was a winner – the theatre, the pub and the Rock Choir members.

In 2012 there occurred the opportunity of a lifetime. The Olympic Games came to London! Whatever else people may think about Tony Blair, his contribution to winning the Olympic bid in the face of all the competition should rank as an achievement of the highest order. Who can forget the scenes of jubilation when the result was announced on 6th July 2005? I was actually in a meeting at the time in Stratford, East London, an area about to be transformed in the following few years by the creation of the Olympic Park.

Jennifer and I had retired by 2012 and happily volunteered with tens of thousands of others to join the 'Gamesmakers' who were afterwards credited with making the 2012 London Games such a joyful and successful event. We duly queued up to get our colourful uniforms and awaited instructions. Jennifer got the most prestigious posting – the Athletes' Village where she rubbed shoulders with the great and the good among the world's top sports people.

My own assignment was slightly less glamorous but turned out to be just as much fun. I was allocated 'soft ticketing'. This meant gathering with other Gamesmakers, often before dawn, to be sent in teams to one of the many entry points to the Olympic Park. We remained outside, and, as the throngs of visitors arrived, our job was to make sure that they were at the right venue on the right day and in possession of the right ticket. It was called soft ticketing because, once we'd checked these general details, they'd go up to the entrance to the Park itself for airport style screening by the Army and the scanning of their tickets to go through.

It was all very good-natured and we developed various bits of banter to get a laugh and create a cheerful impression. The only discordant note I ever encountered during the entire Olympic and Paralympic Games was when a woman angrily remarked that the arrangements were lax because no one had checked her (free) travel pass or her entrance ticket. I pointed out to her – politely I hope – that the tube barriers had been deliberately left open to avoid congestion and that, within a few seconds, the Army would be checking her entrance ticket. I couldn't avoid adding to her fast-disappearing back that this whole complex undertaking had so far gone without a hitch.

One perk we enjoyed as Gamesmakers was that, on the night before the official opening, we got to see a trial run of Danny Boyle's amazing Opening Ceremony. There were notices everywhere telling us not to spread the word on what we'd seen and, as far as I can tell, this must have been complied with because when they saw the event on TV the whole nation was as astonished and delighted as we had been.

2012 also saw the arrival of the first of the grandchildren and, happily, retirement allowed more time to spend with the family. My daughter Emma and her husband Ian saw the birth of Isabelle in January 2012. Their twins Edward and Theo followed in April 2015. My son Joel and his wife Gulistan had Reuben in August 2012 and Raphael in September 2016.

Meanwhile Jennifer's son Jonathan and his wife Hannah were adding to the family with Adaline (Ada) in March 2016 and Joshua in February 2019. Finally (so far) Jennifer's eldest son Benjamin and his wife Holly were delighted by the arrival of their daughter Calliope (Poppy) in May 2020. So, with eight grandchildren aged eight and under by 2020 that meant lots of time with family get-togethers, holidays and school pick-ups.

The grandchildren inevitably provided numerous joyful and entertaining moments – far too many to mention. However, one –which explains the title of this book – sticks in my memory. This was when Jennifer and I took Isabelle and Reuben, aged four or five, for a trip on a vintage railway. They enjoyed the experience enormously and at mid-day we got off the train to have lunch in a stationary carriage which had been converted into a café. After their meal the children asked if they could have ice cream. Jennifer, conscious of family views about healthy eating, said, "I'm not sure your parents would be too pleased". She then popped out to the toilet.

I decided to let the children choose their own desserts with the result that when Jennifer came back she was confronted by the sight of our two young charges eating enormous ice creams. "Good heavens" she said, "I'm not sure that's a good idea". "Well" responded Isabelle, "We're on a special outing – and, anyway, Grandad's a loose cannon". "Who says he's a loose cannon?" asked Jennifer. "Mummy" replied Isabelle. The day continued with the two well-fed children enjoying running up and down the corridors of the ancient train. The turns of phrase – and penetrating insights – of all our grandchildren continue to amuse and delight everyone on a daily basis. They give us enormous pleasure. You can't ask for much more, regardless of what the future holds.

This account of my retirement would be incomplete without an acknowledgement of the positive role played by the Sidcup Rumblers International in my later life. On moving to Eltham in the late 1990's Jennifer and I became good friends with our near neighbours, Alan and Sue Ring.

Among the many activities in which Alan and Sue were involved was the stewardship of a sizeable group of walkers, the core of which comprised Alan's friends, mainly ex-pupils of local grammar schools, but which had been added to over the years and now included me and Jennifer. This group went by the informal title of the Sidcup & District Ramblers and went on country walks punctuated by long and leisurely meals in pubs – or sometimes London walks punctuated by long and leisurely meals in pubs.

On one of the London walks, in the depths of winter, Alan had booked us into a restaurant. He had been there beforehand to discuss the meal and they had agreed to do a special set menu. They asked for a name to print it under. Alan wrote 'The Sidcup and District Rambling Club'. This came out as 'Sidcup and District Rumbling Club' on the printed menu. This gave Alan an excuse to invent a new name. It also emerged that we had been joined by two walkers, not just from the local area but from New Zealand. Clearly, the global reach which had now been achieved required recognition and thus was born the Sidcup Rumblers International.

The Rumblers have provided us with a ready-made circle of friends whose company we have enjoyed in many different settings and who have helped us to establish ourselves in our pleasant corner of southeast London. Sadly we have not made it to New Zealand - yet.

Chapter 16

Reflections

I've never taken to Facebook so I'm grateful that certain resourceful individuals have managed to keep various groups from my past in touch by email. For me these forums include the RAF's 94th Entry, the LSE Socialist Society, the South Africa London Recruits and the MBA course where I met Jennifer.

More recently other email groupings have been added – notably the Sidcup Rumblers (or Ramblers), led by my friend and neighbour Alan Ring, and the South East London Rock Choir, which I joined in retirement. I've also played a role myself in keeping ex-Barking College colleagues in contact through a 'Barking Diners' group and linking together music lovers in Eltham through a database promoting Folk & Blues sessions at the Bob Hope Theatre.

It was the LSE group which led me to look at a 2015 book by Celia Hughes –'Young Lives on the Left' - which contained accounts based on interviews with many of the people I'd known during the heady days of student protest and subsequent far-left political involvement. There were some insights, which got me thinking about my own journey. The book focused on the question of identity – call it self-image.

As a teenager I wanted to be a fighter pilot. Becoming an RAF trainee radio technician was the nearest I got.

I became very close to the 70-odd youngsters thrust together in the 94th Entry and have remained on friendly terms ever since.

In the 1960's I was a student rebel. Marx's predictions of worker-led revolution seemed tantalizingly close during the tumultuous May 1968 events in France and for years afterwards I spent much of my time busily selling the Socialist Worker newspaper and distributing inflammatory leaflets at workplaces and in town centres.

The seemingly unstoppable growth of working class militancy in the 1970's hinted at radical change until it ran into the brick wall of Thatcherite resolve. The 1979 to 1990 government brought its own very different version of radical change. The political landscape was transformed and by the 1990's my earlier activism had given way to a more humble ambition to 'make a difference'. I settled for doing what I could in education and the community. It was in this role – especially my long years at Barking College - that I eventually felt most absorbed and fulfilled.

Various people have influenced my life. Without Mike McKenna I would probably have stayed in the RAF rather than facing a premature departure via a spell in military prison. However, I would not have benefitted from getting into one of the most prestigious universities in the world – the London School of Economics, paving the way for a long-term immersion in far-left politics followed by a subsequent rewarding career in Further Education. And it was at LSE that a conversation with Ronnie Kasrils propelled me into the

South Africa mission, undoubtedly the most hazardous undertaking of my life but one of the most significant.

The reality, I suppose, is that everyone is influenced by others to a degree. Perhaps what matters are the actions which then ensue – and whether there are core values and beliefs which survive these external influences.

In terms of actions, my granddaughter's observation that "Grandad's a loose cannon" remains appropriate. There are aspects of my personality which I was either born with or which developed early in my life. I have often been quick to react both to provocations and opportunities, getting me into trouble on many occasions – but also into taking the lead when circumstances, often unexpected, seemed to require it– perhaps precursors of the more formal leadership roles which materialised in later life.

On the question of values and beliefs I think I have had some which have sustained me through a number of apparently incompatible episodes. The structured and patriotic nature of the RAF seems far removed from the subversive culture of the SWP – yet both require organisational discipline and loyalty. And in both I regarded myself as standing against tyranny and racism. The RAF played a crucial role when Britain stood alone against the Nazis in World War II. The SWP – at least when I was in it – stood against racist organisations at home and oppressive regimes abroad including the Soviet Union and right-wing dictatorships in places such as South Africa, Chile and Portugal.

In view of the significance currently being accorded to the question of identity, whether in relation to race, gender or any other characteristic, it is worth noting the thoughts of Remi Adekoya in his 2021 book 'Biracial Britain' which is based on several interviews with mixed race Britons. The flyleaf states that 'an identity is a story about our life that makes sense to us'. Whilst recognising the importance of community and the need to identify with groups in which we feel comfortable he warns against not allowing our need for belonging to lull us into insular 'groupthink'. He asserts that 'the bravest thing to be is an individual....People sacrifice their individuality to groups too easily....What is important is for us to maintain an individual core that does not wither under the stern gaze of group opinion'.

Despite a nostalgic affection for the friendships and experiences which resulted from the tumultuous days at LSE and its aftermath I find myself somewhat distanced from the left-wing groupthink currently disparaging Britain and its history. My early enforced departure from the RAF didn't stop me thinking that Britain's military could have a positive role to play in world affairs. I have never voted Liberal Democrat but Paddy Ashdown's views on Britain's military responsibilities resonated with me. He was the most prominent politician making the case for NATO intervention to halt the genocide of ethnic Albanians by the Serbs in Kosovo. He also made his opinions clear when the British parliament voted against supporting limited punitive action to stop Assad's chemical attacks on civilians in Syria in April 2013, describing the decision as "the most shameful of my life".

I too was ashamed of Britain – and especially of the Labour Party under its then leader Ed Millband. As a result of Britain's refusal to act, Barack Obama back-tracked on his 'red line' regarding the use of chemical weapons - so nothing was done and the conditions persisted for the continuing horrors in Syria, the dramatic expansion of Islamic State as a focus of opposition to Assad and, in due course, the intervention of Russia in support of Assad.

When Russia began bombing civilians and wiping out rebel cities there was not so much as a whimper of opposition from the Left in Britain, in contrast to the orchestrated mass protests against the West's proposed bombing of Assad's military bases. There has been similar left-wing silence over Russian expansionism and its use of murder squads to silence critics. Throughout much of the world there is a thirst for democracy. Whenever I see images of the oppressed confronting lines of riot police I know which side I am on. However, disapproval of tyrannical regimes abroad need not blind us to injustices at home.

In Britain the Labour Party was once the voice of the dispossessed. No longer. In the December 2019 General Election the Labour Party's working-class base defected en masse to the Tories, albeit possibly half-heartedly. We now, bizarrely, have a Labour Party with a predominantly middle-class membership whilst the majority of the working class votes Tory. A 2020 book by Paul Embery, 'Despised: why the Modern Left loathes the Working Class' points to a possible way back for the Labour Party, but only if it can bring itself to embrace traditional 'red wall' values of family, community and country. Paul Embery makes his case from the perspective of a Labour Party and trade union activist brought up on the Becontree housing estate in solidly working class Barking & Dagenham:-

Post-industrial, small-town and coastal communities have been ignored for too long by an arrogant cultural and liberal elite which has seen those who inhabit those places and their patriotic and traditional values as backward, benighted and a drag on the nation's inexorable journey to the sunlit uplands of cosmopolitan liberalism.

The reckoning was a long time coming but, when it came, it came with a roar. The UK is out of the EU, the Red Wall has crumbled, and the labour movement stands marginalised from the mainstream of society.

This cry from Barking & Dagenham brings me back to my long sojourn at Barking College.   Politics were involved from time to time – the stand against the British National Party was an example – but the essential role of the place was to deliver high quality and vocationally relevant education and training to local people – eventually hundreds of thousands during my time there. This was achieved by hundreds of dedicated staff – lecturers and support staff - who together shared a common commitment to serving local people to the best of their ability. In doing so they provided generations of local people, from one of the most deprived areas of London, with the skills and knowledge which enabled them to develop pride in their achievements, to make a decent living and to build careers and businesses.

The Celia Hughes book mentioned at the start of this chapter reminded me quite forcefully of the years of activism during which my life was dominated by the demands of the SWP – up in the morning selling the Socialist Worker newspaper at factory gates, weekends spent on demonstrations, weekly branch meetings planning various events and interventions. I regret, echoing the sentiments of several others mentioned in the book, that all this frenetic activity led me to neglect both my original family back in Folkestone and my first marriage.

Family is fundamental – something I didn't properly appreciate until I had children of my own. Caring for them became all-consuming and hugely rewarding. The importance of family was further reinforced when a subsequent generation of lively and inventive grandchildren came along. This family focus has increasingly put into perspective the time I had previously spent on political activism. There were episodes of which I remain proud. But much of what I did was unproductive time-wasting.

I'm not sure therefore whether I'd be the best person to offer advice to a rising generation. All things considered I've made plenty of mistakes. But I suppose I'd be fairly safe in suggesting that time devoted to the family is never wasted – and that if you can get a good balance between family life and making a decent contribution outside, whether in paid work, political involvement or voluntary community action, you can regard yourself as having got something right. Families and communities are the building blocks of a decent society.

Fortunately our children have set up home fairly near to where Jennifer and I are living so it's possible to stay in touch with them, usually seeing them every week and getting everyone together for various family occasions. I've been through some turbulent times and taken many false turns but I feel that, despite this, some of what I did was worthwhile and in the end I made a useful contribution. No doubt I could have done better – future generations of the family certainly will, despite the inevitable challenges and occasional stumbles.

Printed in Great Britain
by Amazon